Hegel In His Time

Hegel
In His Time

Jacques D'Hondt

translated by
John Burbidge

with Nelson Roland and Judith Levasseur

broadview press

Cataloguing in Publication Data

Hondt, Jacques D'
   Hegel in his time

Translation of: Hegel en son temps.
ISBN 0-921149-16-6

1. Hegel, Georg Wilhelm Friedrich, 1770-1831.
2. Philosophers- Germany- Biography. I. Title.

B2947.H6613 1988   193   C87-095156-4

58,645

Copyright© 1988, Broadview Press Ltd.

in Canada:
broadview press
PO Box 1243
Peterborough, Ont. K9J 7H5

in the United States:
broadview press
421 Center St.
Lewiston, NY 14092

Printed in Canada by Gagné Ltd.

This book has been published with the help of a grant from the Canadian Federation of the Humanities, using funds provided by the Social Sciences and Humanities Research Council of Canada.

Contents

Preface
by H.S. Harris

To speak of "Hegel's time" is to utter a riddle. For it was Hegel's fortune to live in two widely different times. The Bastille was stormed when he was nineteen; and all of his early work was done under the shadow of the Revolution, and of Napoleon. His two great books, the *Phenomenology of Spirit* and the *Science of Logic*, belong properly to the Napoleonic age – though the last of the three volumes of the *Science of Logic* appeared only after Waterloo. So, with the advantage of hindsight, we can fairly say that "Hegel's time" was that of the French Emperor who was only a year older than he.

In that first time however, when he did his most important work, Hegel remained almost invisible. Only one or two enthusiastic students might have said then that the time was "his". It was after Napoleon was dead and buried on St. Helena that Hegel became almost as visible and as predominant in his own sphere as the Emperor had been in the political world before 1815. The paradox is that that later time, which belonged to Hegel in the eyes of the public, could never belong to him *in the Spirit*, because he was a true contemporary of Napoleon.

Jacques D'Hondt's book *Hegel in his Time* deals with, and documents, this paradox. Hegel at Berlin, the dominant figure in what was then, without dispute, the intellectual capital of the world, was still, as D'Hondt says, "in hiding". Behind the facade of the great philosophy professor, soon to be Rector Magnificus of the University for his appointed term, there was still the committed believer in a Napoleonic "new order". Invited to dine with the Crown Prince and Princess of Prussia in 1830, the stiff and awkward Rector became a different person when the

Princess (born Marianne von Hessen-Homburg) mentioned Hölderlin. As Princess Marianne recorded in her diary and family letters, the time and place (Homburg vor der Hohe, 1799-1800) and her elder sister's love for the poet were at once brought vividly to life again in her mind. I am sure that they said nothing about revolutionary politics at that Court dinner-table, but the political background of Hölderlin's mental breakdown must also have been alive again in Hegel's memory then and there.

D'Hondt is well placed to write about the hidden aspect of Hegel's career in Berlin; for in *Hegel secret* (Paris, P.U.F., 1968) he did pioneer work in exposing the revolutionary commitments and sympathies of Hegel and his friends from their student days onwards. Much in Hegel's life was always necessarily a secret from the general public, and D'Hondt has shown himself to be an expert in identifying the hints and enigmatic references in the surviving papers which are our pointers to that secret life. In the Berlin years (as the reader will soon see) much more of the evidence is part of the public record. But it has been passed over, and its significance has not been grasped, because Hegel's own position and statements as a public servant created a smokescreen around it.

We must, of course, beware of over-simplification. The professor at Berlin is no longer the young revolutionary of whom Sinclair — another close friend at the court of Homburg at the turn of the century — said that in the flow of his political oratory he had a "flaming sword" at his command. It was not *fear*, but the agonizing effort to rise above all passions and observe the world logically in pure thought, that deprived Hegel of his flaming sword, and made his lecturing style a byword for its stumbling painfulness. As a professor he wanted to be beyond and above both revolution and reaction. He was still a secret radical in ethics and religion — a fact divined by some of his most brilliant students, notably Ludwig Feuerbach and Heinrich Heine. But this philosophical radicalism was not basically political, and in his struggle after a "Scientific", or objectively open-eyed, awareness of how the human world really is, Hegel resembles Freud more than Marx (though his ideal of "science" is socio-historical rather than psychological, and Freud is *not* like Marx, one of his true heirs).

D'Hondt, of course, is close to Marx in his sympathies. He writes here as a counsel for the defence on behalf of the *Privatdozent* of thirty-five, whose lectures at Jena contained several anticipations of the later Marxist critique of bourgeois society. D'Hondt is quite frank and open about this; he takes it for granted that everyone already knows the "myth" that he is critically overthrowing. And it is safe to assume that everyone who knows anything about Hegel knows the myth. From Schopenhauer to Karl Popper, a century later, it has enjoyed a long life already.

We must remember, however, that myths are powerful and persistent because they contain important truths (however distorted). The reader of this book will see an important myth decisively overthrown and exploded. If (s)he reads Popper's chapter on Hegel (in the second volume of the *Open Society and its Enemies*) before or afterwards (s)he will know, beyond a doubt, which picture is closer to the truth. But that knowledge is only the first step. Everything – including many fragments of the exploded myth – must be picked up and put together again in a new picture. We shall, in fact, find ourselves with a whole gallery of new pictures; for we shall never be able to agree perfectly about the *rational* shape of Hegel's actual career at Berlin. How far a given utterance is motivated by prudence, and how far by conviction will never be settled. In the end, as Hegel taught already in the *Phenomenology*, those who seek to comprehend the rationality of the actual must give up being moral valets. We must accept the record *as a whole*, with an honest recognition of its ambiguities.

D'Hondt himself is that paradoxical being, the moral valet whose master is still for him a hero. It is this generosity of spirit that makes his book the first that we ought to read about the world-historical professor. So we should be glad to have it here before us, rendered into clear and supple English by John Burbidge and his helpers. But D'Hondt himself is a good Hegelian. He wants us to have, and to comprehend, the record as a whole. So we must also rejoice that we do now, at last, have a complete translation of Hegel's *Letters* (by Clark Butler and Christiane Seiler, Univ. of Indiana Press, 1984). Unlike the French edition, it does not contain most of the letters *to* Hegel; and only in German, as yet, do we have an adequate collection of the opinions and recollections of Hegel's contemporaries about him. These are the essential sources to which we must go, when we seek to construct a properly comprehensive image of Hegel the man, in what was indeed "his time". But there is no better place to begin than with Jacques D'Hondt's brief for the defence.

H.S. Harris
Glendon College, York University, Toronto

INTRODUCTION

Jacques D'Hondt's Hegel

Hegel's philosophy can best be described as a dilemma. On the one hand it purports to be an absolute system, which has transcended every relative or partial standpoint. On the other hand, it contains a method and way of reasoning that turns every confident assertion upside down and disrupts anything that resists change.

In the texts that remain, Hegel seems to juggle both these features in a single, comprehensive theory. Those who tried to learn from him found it impossible to follow his example. Some affirmed the system as a totality that remained impervious to change; in that case the dialectic became simply a technique used to disperse challenges to its dominance, ensuring that nothing new would ever emerge. Others affirmed the method of internal decay, external challenge, and transformation into opposites; when this method was applied to Hegel's system itself, its presumptuous pride tumbled into ruins.*

---

*Lawrence S. Stepelvich has collected some of the writings of Hegel's disciples in *The Young Hegelians, An Anthology* (Cambridge, 1983). J.E. Toews, *Hegelianism, The Path Toward Dialectical Humanism, 1805-1841* (Cambridge, 1980) discusses the intellectual history of the period in some detail.

Hegelians, then, are either right wing or left. Either Hegel has in principle said everything in a static absolute, or Hegel has destroyed himself by way of a magnificent *reductio ad absurdum*.

These two schools formed soon after Hegel's death, and they have continued to the present. Both not only ask "Where do we go after Hegel?", but also return to Hegel himself and inquire into his own position. Did Hegel lean to the right or to the left? Was Hegel dissolving all particularity into an all-encompassing absolute in the manner of Plotinus (J.N. Findlay) or Spinoza (E.E. Harris)? Or is his thought inherently revolutionary (Marx), his particular judgements the conditioned product of his time (Kierkegaard)?

The view of Hegel as a left wing thinker *seems* much harder to defend. For Hegel concludes each of his major works with a chapter on absolutes: absolute knowledge; the absolute idea; absolute spirit. And Hegel ended his life in one of the centres of post-Napoleonic reaction, as professor of philosophy at the University of Berlin. As a result left-wing Hegelians, such as Kojève, have been led to caricature Hegel as saying that history stopped once he finished writing the *Phenomenology of Spirit*; and the foolishness of the caricature allows the balance of Hegel's theory, with its dialectic and change, to remain as alone worth considering.

Hegel's writing is so dense and difficult that we can always find some texts to support our interpretations. The secondary literature is full of a kind of "cutting and pasting". Congenial paragraphs are stressed; difficult complications are either explained away or ignored. Invariably interpreters have moulded Hegel into their own image.

The contemporary French philosopher, Jacques D'Hondt, has found a way out of this impasse. D'Hondt takes his place on the left wing. He belongs to the school of Hegel interpreters that sees him through the eyes of Engels and the young Marx. For all that Marx and Engels have gone beyond Hegel in stressing the material basis of the dialectical process, they were able to do so because they stood on his shoulders.

There have been others who have adopted this interpretative model. D'Hondt's approach is distinctive because he does not confine himself to Hegel's published remains, but sets Hegel in his historical setting. He looks for the writers that influenced him; he discovers those acts that betray fundamental convictions and beliefs. If we know the sources Hegel was using and if we can point to the way he put his thoughts into practice, we then have evidence that will help us distance interpretation from simple conjecture or arbitrary selection.

Hegel was a man of his time. He knew what science had discovered; he read the literature that was then available. It provided the raw material which he could then refine into his philosophy. His ideas, then, did not exist in a vacuum; they were a reflection of the age in which they were thought. And they will be understood only when placed within that historical setting.

So D'Hondt practises philosophy by undertaking an historical investigation. In this book, *Hegel in his time*, he sets Hegel into the political world of the 1820's. As central Europe became more rigid under the post-Napoleonic reaction, here was someone who avoided the excesses of romantic patriotism, yet was prepared to take a stand for freedom of expression and constitutional reform.

That this reflected a long-standing conviction, D'Hondt has shown in other writings. *Hegel secret* documents the young Hegel's familiarity with the writing of French Girondins, the liberal advocates of constitutional government. Whenever the young tutor, who was eking out a living until he could return to academic pursuits, arrived in a strange town, he soon established contact with people known to be active in the most progressive strands of the Masonic order, with its concern for enlightenment through education and universal brotherhood. He avidly read the journals they published, even though their liberal ideas were considered subversive by the authorities. With lengthy quotations D'Hondt illustrates how themes espoused by Volnay, Rabaut, L.S. Mercier and George Forster, all active in one way or another in the French Revolution, were picked up almost verbatim in Hegel's writings and lectures. When a person is found appropriating such ideas, even though he does not name his sources lest he be tarred as dangerous himself, that person is in no way a conservative or reactionary. The interpreter is justified in finding the theme of progress and change through destruction and decay as the basic thrust of Hegel's writing.

D'Hondt takes Hegel out of the atemporal world of eternally valid ideas and sets him back into the years of Napoleon and the French Revolution, of the Enlightenment interest in nature and travel. It is this age that Hegel brings to expression in his theories of history, science, art, religion and philosophy. And when he moves on to the more abstract discussions of logic, these pure thoughts too are but the distilled essence of their time; they summarize the accumulated wisdom of human experience. Philosophy cannot leap into a transhistorical sphere in which the future is known in principle, if not in detail.

In recognizing that Hegel's ideas cannot be divorced from his time, D'Hondt is simply following his master. In his most important work, *Hegel, philosophe de l'histoire vivante*, D'Hondt has investigated Hegel's philosophy of history. Central to his analysis is the role of chance. History, for Hegel, is not the sphere of causal necessity. It is bedevilled with contingency. Things simply happen; people have to react to unexpected events. Events and reaction work on each other to create a complex social network. Then the philosopher comes on the scene, and notices how the reciprocal relations that bind the various elements are themselves the products of their mutual interaction. In this way he shows that they are the necessary components of a single totality. Although initially not necessary, they become so through the effects they produce, and the changes introduced into them by subsequent events.

Where chance has a major role to play in establishing what becomes true, there can be no perspective of eternity. Philosophies are the products of their times, summarizing the network of contingent conditions that made up the cumulative experience of their age. The more they include of the past, the more comprehensive their view of the present. But they cannot foretell the future.

Indeed, there is an inherent irony in their own achievement. For philosophers can comprehend their time only by removing themselves from it. The contingent events that make up an age must have slipped into the past; the immediate reactions, both passionate and reflective, by which people transform such events into cultural reality, will also be part of history. Thought comprehends the totality of its age only after that age has passed its zenith. The network of reciprocity can be grasped only when it is complete; when life has matured.

Because thought directed at grasping the total picture is no longer a part of that picture, a rupture has been introduced into history. The very effort to be all-comprehensive destroys the totality, for it tears itself away from the fabric of the present and past. In making their thought public, philosophers thus break with their age. Their theories become in turn the focus of action and reaction; they generate new contingencies. In the very act of recognizing the continuities that integrate a moment of time into a thickly woven fabric of human life, philosophy introduces a rupture. Things can no longer be the same.

D'Hondt points out that here Hegel was offering a philosophical history rather than a philosophy of history. Even in his lectures on art, religion and philosophy, Hegel explored the way in which a specific historical context moulded an age; and he went on to show that even the decline and fall of past civilizations was part of the collective memory that defined the present life of later generations.

For D'Hondt the real Hegel is to be found in the incomplete sketches of youth and the ever revised lectures of the Berlin years. In the spoken word and in written fragments nothing is finalized; everything is open to the future. This is why Hegel's last major works, the *Encyclopaedia of the Philosophical Sciences* and the *Philosophy of Right* are not treatises in their own right, but sets of theses for lectures. They are to be completed by the spoken word that passes away as soon as it is expressed. But Hegel has been betrayed by the *Phenomenology of Spirit* and the *Science of Logic*. Although the former retains a sense of history, the latter has transmuted life into the ashes of pure thought. The dynamic of change has been crystallized into an arid dance of concepts. Time has been made to stand still in some realm of pure essence.

However, D'Hondt has no need to cut and paste. For he applies Hegel's dialectical view of history to Hegel himself. The system of absolute idealism, no less than the philosophies Hegel himself discusses in his lectures, summarizes an age, introduces a break with the past, and triggers actions and reactions. Hegelianism as a whole comes to be outmoded.

But, peculiarly enough, in becoming outmoded its vision of the dialectic is confirmed. For this idealism has itself been subjected to historical transformation. Challenged by the materialism of Marx and Engels it has retreated into the past. But it has not disappeared into outright falsehood. For it is now a central component of human experience. And subsequent generations must incorporate it into their cultural memory if they are to understand themselves.

At this point D'Hondt takes his stand against Althusser's Marxism. Inspired by structuralism, Althusser had taken Marx's theory as an independent package, distinct from those of both Hegel and Engels: dialectic, life and change – the process of historical development – were set aside and replaced by structural affinities. D'Hondt responded by documenting the revolutionary influences on Hegel, by showing that the historical Hegel, for all his pettiness, was active in supporting progressive individuals against state repression, by discerning the positive assessments that Marx and Engels made of their predecessor in the midst of their polemics against him, by recognizing that these polemics were themselves historically situated. In all this, he not only demonstrated that the historical relations were far more complicated than Althusser's theory would admit, but he expressed and exemplified the kind of philosophy that is now required. One can no longer develop a priori systems, whether idealist or structuralist. One must look to the dynamic of history, and discover there the reciprocal influence of thought and action.

There is a paradox in what D'Hondt is doing. Despite his claim that Hegel's system as a whole is outdated, he adopts Hegel's understanding of history and historical change. D'Hondt has applied to Hegel's own system the kind of analysis and description that Hegel applied to his predecessors. There is a reciprocal relation between theory and its context: the context sets the conditions for thought; thought by transmuting life into the realm of pure essence marks the end of an era; and life reacts in turn to this resumé of its past by creating new and unanticipated events. In rejecting Hegelianism and moving on to something else D'Hondt has confirmed it.

He does so by setting Hegel into his time. The man who

wrote the *Science of Logic* was anxious about making ends meet, his personal life frequently verging on disaster. The *Phenomenology*, with its lengthy and arduous process of initiation, came at a time when Hegel was frequenting the company of known Masons, some of them graduates of the banned Illuminati. The *Philosophy of Right* urged a constitutional monarchy in a capital city where the king had reneged on his promise to grant a constitution. And its author earned the king's ire for more petty reasons as well. Only when the completed texts are recognized as partial and set within the context of spoken comments, committed actions, and constant reading does one begin to appreciate their real significance.

When interpreted as a man of his time, Hegel himself turns out to be left wing. But D'Hondt is not claiming that Hegel's philosophy sets a perennial standard against which all subsequent thought is to be assessed. For Hegelianism is a feature of the past, of the early years of the nineteenth century. And like all comprehensive philosophy it ruptured the continuity of past and present. It was a radical moment of negation that propelled history into a new age. In accordance with his own principles, Hegel heralds the post-Hegelian era. He prepares the ground for Marx's materialism.

No negation, however, is absolute. Contraries become contradictories. And contradictions appear as such only because both sides are held together in a single perspective. Therefore the dialectical rupture leads on to a renewed community, a renewed perspective of totality. The contradictories are recognized as mutually conditioning each other. Hegel's thought is seen as the product of its world, and that world is in turn moulded by his intellectual influence. This reciprocal relation becomes the next philosophical discovery.

As D'Hondt says, one cannot learn from the past. After Hegel, history can no longer be regarded as philosophy taught by examples. Each relation of conditioning is specific, moulded by change, governed by the distinctive (and contingent) issues that have emerged. What happens in history will not happen again. But what one does learn is that thought and the world cannot be divorced from each other – that any philosophical comprehension will describe the way one stimulates and moulds the other. And by understanding how this happened in the past, one makes it live in the present.

By practising this kind of philosophy and by showing how it is rooted in Hegel's own writing and speaking, Jacques D'Hondt shows himself to be, not a valet in the cause of philosophical history, but one of its key protagonists.

John Burbidge

JACQUES D'HONDT

Born at Tours in 1920, Jacques D'Hondt undertook philosophical studies at the University of Poitiers. Deported to Germany as a civilian labourer during the World War, he became interested in German thought, and came under the influence of Jean Hyppolite. Appointed to the University of Poitiers, he founded in 1970 the Centre for Research and Documentation on Hegel and Marx. Elected president of La Société Française de Philosophie in 1981, he continued to teach in Poitiers until his retirement in 1985.

Hegel, philosophe de l'histoire vivante. Presses universitaires de France [Series: Épiméthée] 1966, 2nd edition, 1987. (Spanish translation, Buenos Aires, 1971.)

Hegel, sa vie, son oeuvre, sa philosophie. Presses universitaires de France [Series: Sup-philosophes] 1967, 2nd edition, 1975. (Portugese translation, Lisbon, 1981.)

Hegel secret, Recherches sur les sources cachées de la pensée de Hegel. Presses universitaires de France [Series: Épiméthée] 1968, 2nd edition, 1986. (German translation, Berlin, 1972 & 1983; Japanese translation, Tokyo, 1980; Spanish translation, Buenos Aires, 1976.)

Hegel en son temps (Berlin 1818-1831). Editions Sociales [Series: Problèmes] 1968. (German translation, Berlin, 1973 & 1984; Italian translation, Naples, 1979; Japanese translation, Tokyo, 1983.)

De Hegel à Marx. Presses universitaires de France [Series: Bibliothèque de philosophie contemporaine] 1972. (Spanish translation, Buenos Aires, 1974.)

L'idéologie de la rupture. Presses universitaires de France [Series: Philosophie d'aujourd'hui] 1978. (Spanish translation, Mexico, 1983.)

Hegel et hégélianisme. Presses universitaires de France [Series: Que sais-je?] 1982, 2nd edition, 1986. (Portugese translation, Lisbon, 1984.)

Hegel, le philosophe du débat et du combat. Librairie Générale Française [Series: Le Livre de Poche] 1984.

D'Hondt's only other publication in English is his article: "On Rupture and Destruction in History," *Clio* xv 4, pp 345-358.

The translator's notes, indicated in the text by an asterisk (*), will be found on pages 211ff.

Hegel In His Time

Foreword

Hegel is still in hiding.

Only with difficulty are we tearing our eyes away from a portrait painted long ago. At that time certain facts had not been noticed; some manuscripts had not come to light; and judgments were based on criteria now out of date.

As historical distance increases, our perspective expands, objective data accumulate, and the publication of Hegel's manuscripts and lectures continues. Despite the changed value of the documents on which they were based, however, the old summary condemnations are still applied. Scholars persist in viewing Hegel as a 'servile bureaucrat,' as a 'defender of the Prussian order', and sometimes even as a 'reactionary'. They go to the point of denouncing — as an ultimate sin — his Prussian 'chauvinism'.

A traditional view, to be sure, but a false one. In the Prussian capital Hegel is supposed to have 'arrived', to have become a person of consequence, happy and content with the society in which he thrived. As official philosopher, he is said to have prostituted his talents in the service of an absolute monarchy, which covered him with honours. His works reputedly provided the political and social reaction with a set of complaisant theoretical justifications.

Several accusers have gone so far as to claim that Hegel was the accomplice of the police and pointed out reformers to them.

On what basis are such judgments made?

Almost exclusively on Hegel's own writings, and in particular on certain passages from his *Elements of the Philosophy of Right*. This volume of Hegel's works is taken in isolation, and accorded the status of the master's last word. It is then interpreted tendentiously by focusing on several paragraphs that seem scandalous. As a final blow, those who dismiss Hegel's *Philosophy of Right* do not take the trouble to situate it in its historical context.

Treated in this way Hegel's political doctrine acquires a regressive, or at least a conservative, character. A hasty generalization leads to the conclusion: as the doctrine, so the man. And the axe falls.

Certainly those who characterize the *Philosophy of Right* as reactionary through and through commit a great injustice; and several authors have recently endeavoured to make this point.

Our purpose is not to support their conclusion by further analyses of texts — analyses whose utility and urgency we do not question. We prefer, instead, to look *around* the text. We shall clarify Hegel's actual political stance in Berlin through a close consideration of his concrete situation in the circumstances of precisely that time and place.

When a thinker cannot publish everything he thinks, we have to look for his thoughts in sources other than his publications. The Prussia of 1820 was under the controls and censorship of a feudal monarchy. A philosopher had to hold back from saying everything. To express his real sentiments he had to use means other than the printing press.

This is why we say that Hegel had three philosophies of right.

The first is the one he published and exposed to the attacks of his enemies, which had difficulty in penetrating the barricades of censorship.

Second is the one his intellectual friends and disciples read between the lines of the published text, fleshing it out with the spoken comments the master was making at the same time, and taking note of the changes of direction imposed on him by events and occasions — constraints to which they also were subjected.

Finally, there is the philosophy of right whose maxims Hegel actually followed in his daily life. We shall decipher the practical commitments that in fact took up Hegel's time, to show how he dealt with the reality of the institutions whose theory he expounded: trade and commerce, marriage and family, civil society, administration, the state; and also how they dealt with him.

Over the years, however, trinities have had a habit of becoming one. Taken together, Hegel's three philosophies of right do not contradict each other. They unite to support each other. A single spirit gives them life. They move in the same direction, but to a greater or lesser extent. It is in his actions that Hegel shows himself to be the most intrepid and, as one would expect, the most dynamic.

To get to know the man a little better, we shall have recourse to his private writings, to what survives of his invaluable correspondence. But perhaps what does not survive would have been the most revealing. Of necessity, certain of his letters would have been destroyed by their recipients.

As well, we shall gather together the testimonies of his contemporaries; we shall assemble external evidence and generally everything that will enable us to establish, by inference and comparison, the conditions in which he actually lived, thought and acted.

Hegel's first biographers knew nothing about the bulk of the documents we will be using. Is it necessary to recall that even the important texts collected under the title *Hegel's Early Theological Writings* were not published until 1907, more than seventy years after the philosopher's death?

This extraordinary delay helps us understand the inevitably tentative and hypothetical character of judgments made in earlier days about a man of whom were known neither the complete works nor the private life.

Even though a number of details are certainly still lacking, Hegel's dossier now allows us to offer a more faithful picture of the philosopher. An initial observation is justified: almost everything that has come forward to augment the record in the last fifty years serves to accentuate the progressive character of Hegel's political approach and to 'nuance', as they say, its conservative features.

The latter are well known and indisputable. It should be understood that our purpose is to display the unknown Hegel: the anxious man, the stubborn citizen, the friend of the persecuted.

PART ONE

Hegel's Situation

I

The Career

For a start, let us destroy the legend of a Hegel who was secure, favoured by fate, his personal existence protected from all difficulties and problems.

The conservative usually seeks to maintain above all else his own well-being, his material and moral comfort. Hegel would pass more easily as a conservative if his stay at Berlin had actually matched the description of it Roques recently offered:

> After years of material uncertainty, or of quite modest existence, he is now in a situation as splendid as his dreams: he is in favour at court and very powerful; he enjoys affection at home; he has friends as well as several enthusiastic admirers; each year his birthday is a triumph.[1]

Not a single statement in that passage is completely true.

Is it even fair to say, as someone has said recently, that "the life of this academic with his brilliant career involved no particularly noteworthy events"?[2]

Brilliant career? A career certainly slow in coming!

Hegel's arrival in Berlin is pictured simply as a coronation, a consummation, and a consecration. In fact it was just as much a beginning, a tentative probe.

Hegel finished revising the *Philosophy of Right* some time in 1820. It appeared in 1821. We might easily imagine the philosopher, now in his fifties and surrounded with respect and unanimous admiration, being simply interested in preserving the lustre of a reputation already acquired. His fame rested on works like the *Phenomenology*, the *Logic*, and the *Encyclopaedia*. Avid disciples defended him. Soon he would assume important positions in the university.

But this provides only a partial view of things; one which is partial in both senses, as looking at only a part, and as taking a one-sided or tendentious approach.

When he received his nomination to Berlin, Hegel had taught with the rank of university professor for just two years. Only in October 1816, aged 46, did he finally begin an academic career at Heidelberg—for one cannot legitimately count the several years previously spent at Jena, first as *Privatdozent*, lacking any official remuneration, then as "professor extraordinary" at a stipend of one hundred thalers a year!

Into these delayed beginnings, the nomination to Berlin added a further rupture. To be sure it offered a promotion—quite a flattering one—but it required an emigration as well.

Those of us who are French, familiar with the customs and laws of a unitary state, would naturally imagine this change in Hegel's life to be like the transfer of a professor from one university to another, from Strassburg, for example, to Paris. But in the Germany of that time it had a completely different significance. Berlin and Heidelberg were certainly situated in the same country—the focus of heart-felt yearning on the part of German patriots. But they were attached to it only as an ideal, and feared it might never be realized.

In 1818 Heidelberg belonged to one state: the grand-duchy of Baden; and Berlin to another: the kingdom of Prussia. For Hegel, Berlin represented the final stage in a long international itinerary.

Let us follow the path of this wandering, unfortunate and rootless philosopher, of this patriot deprived of a native land. Born and educated in Württemberg, he avoided taking a position there. Together with Hölderlin and Schelling he shared an aversion to the life they had led at the Tübingen *Stift*, the Protestant seminary where they had all studied.

Hegel could have become a tutor or a teacher at the *Stift*. But Hölderlin expressed their shared opinion about that:

> Only once we are on the point of splitting wood or selling boot polish and hair cream let us ask if there might not perhaps be something better: being a tutor in Tübingen.[3]

To such an unpleasant and, according to him, humiliating situation, Hegel preferred a long and difficult pilgrimage in search of the promised land, marked with numerous way stations: Berne, Frankfurt, Jena, Bamberg, Nürnberg, Heidelberg, Berlin.

The different occupations and new beginnings were almost as numerous as the frontiers crossed: tutor, private teacher, lecturer, editor and publisher of a newspaper, headmaster of a secondary school, and finally university professor – but not until 1816.

In contrast, the close friend of his youth, Schelling, named professor at Jena in 1798, had taught in a university since the age of 23, eighteen years earlier than the older Hegel. His "intimate enemy", Fries, had started his university teaching career eleven years earlier in 1805, aged 32. Younger men had acquired positions while he, Hegel, knowing himself to be the superior scholar, lagged behind, forgotten and despised.

He was also poor. A bursary student of the Grand Duchy of Württemberg at Tübingen, as so many sons of modest families, he found himself forced by lack of funds to take the position of private tutor for six years. After this long trial, a small inheritance allowed him several years respite at Jena, leisure for study. Without the death of his father, would he ever have found the opportunity to write the *Phenomenology*?

The parental legacy was quickly exhausted, however, and until 1816, Hegel looked doggedly and almost hopelessly for a good position with a regular salary, but without success.

Several times he fell into the utmost penury, having to use the guarantee of his friends to borrow sums of money that he would subsequently repay only with difficulty.

After the battle of Jena, during which his apartment was plundered, he had nothing to live on, and when Goethe discovered his distress, he asked Knebel to give him ten thalers!* Later Niethammer* agreed to serve as his guarantor with the publisher of the *Phenomenology*. In 1811, the date of his marriage barely missed being postponed because funds were lacking.[4] And once married, Hegel wrote the *Science of Logic* very quickly, not in response to an irrepressible philosophical inspiration, but so that he could sell the manuscript sooner, and thus improve the precarious financial situation of his household.[5]

We can easily understand his rejoicing when he was named to Berlin. Sweet revenge! At one stroke he acquired comfort as well as fame.

However, he did not at the same time achieve *security*. Hegel was not an optimist, as people have often falsely thought, nor even phlegmatic; he was always anxious, as he himself recognized clearly enough.[6] And events only served to feed this anxiety.

As we shall see, Hegel did not live a single year in Berlin without experiencing legitimate apprehensions. His insecure position was threatened by political incidents in which he found himself implicated, by the arbitrariness and caprice of power, by the unexpected consequences of certain features in his private life, and by the boldness both of his teaching and of the interpretations given to it by the public.

Openly or in secret, many powerful enemies attacked him. With a clear eye he saw the perils increase; he anticipated having to seek sanctuary.

When the vicar of *Saint Hedwig's* accused him of violating the Catholic faith in his courses and he had to provide a written justification to his superiors, he was probably sensitive to his own vulnerability more than ever. Taking the measure of his adversaries' thrusts and the barely sufficient resistance of his protectors, Hegel, at fifty-seven, seriously considered the likelihood of a new departure, the prospect of exiling himself once again.

In August 1827 he made a trip to Paris, partly to escape the perils that his presence in Berlin at that time would create. But his stay in the French capital itself fed suspicion.

As he passed through Belgium on his return from France, he visited several towns in the company of his student and friend, van Ghert, a Dutch civil servant who had already offered his assistance several times.* At that time he wrote to his wife:

In Liège as in Louvain and Ghent there are beautiful university buildings. We have looked these universities over as a prospective resting place in case the priests in Berlin make *Küpfergraben*[7] completely unbearable for me. The Curia in Rome would in any event be a more honorable adversary than the inanities of an inane clericalism in Berlin.[8]

Often Hegel had to take precautions, to withdraw tentative initiatives, and to manoeuvre. He could never consider his professional position to be finally secure, and nothing could be more illusory than to compare it, in this regard, to that of even the most insignificant civil servant of our own day, whose rights are guaranteed by statute, or at least set out in a regulation, and who, once an injustice is committed against him, can count on the support of his colleagues.

It is difficult to determine exactly what Hegel's financial position was at Berlin. The style of life in those days differed from that in ours, and as a result the expenditures were not of the same order. In addition the German currency was not the same in the various states; even in a single state the percentage of precious metal in the coinage, and thus its absolute value, varied from region to region.[9]

Forced to keep accounts, Hegel has himself left a number of indications of his salary, his income, his expenditures. Because of them we can at least get a measure of the scale of his finances, and make comparisons with that of his colleagues.

The appointment to Berlin was accompanied by a significant increase in his salary, which from then on amounted to 2,000 thalers a year, not counting various honoraria for supplementary services. The increase over his Heidelberg salary, however, was not as great as it seemed.

In a letter to his sister, Hegel himself remarked that, in considering the difference in salaries it was necessary to take particular note of the local purchasing power, and of the cost of living. He estimated that the 2,000 Prussian thalers actually equalled 2,000 florins. At Heidelberg he had received 1,500 florins.[10]

A significant difference to be sure, but the two successive salaries only made possible the same standard of living. The "philosopher of the state", "the dictator of the Prussian university" did not receive the stipend that those titles would suggest.

His life continued to be quite modest.

He frequently complained of the uncertainty of his "economic circumstances".[11] Nor could he take trips to recover his health, to relax, or to do research, without obtaining a special grant from the ministry.[12]

Hegel was not more favourably treated than his colleagues at the University of Berlin. Several of them earned more than 2,000 thalers. According to Geiger, the highest salaries accrued to medical doctors and chemists (between 1,500 and 2,000 thalers), to theologians (between 2,000 and 2,500 thalers), and to jurists (between 2,500 and 3,000 thalers).[13]

Nor was he more privileged than the philosophers of his standing in other countries. Jacobi, at Munich, received a salary of 3,000 thalers.

To obtain an adequate estimate of the value ascribed to intelligence in Berlin at the beginning of the nineteenth century, it may be worth while to recall that the civil list of King Frederick William III amounted to 2,500,000 thalers.

And on Hegel's death, the crown prince insisted that Schelling be offered a salary of 6,000 thalers to entice him to Berlin to combat Hegelianism[14]

NOTES

1. P. Roques, *Hegel, sa vie et ses oeuvres*, (Paris, 1912) 351.

2. P. Touilleux, *Introduction aux systèmes de Marx et de Hegel* (Paris, n.d.) 3; see also page 6.

3. *Briefe von und an Hegel*, ed. J. Hoffmeister, (Berlin, 1970), Vol. I, p. 41. Henceforth we will refer to this edition of Hegel's correspondence by the short title: *Briefe*. Where appropriate, reference will also be made to the English edition of Hegel's letters, *Hegel: The Letters*, translated by Clark Butler and Christiane Seiler, (Bloomington, Indiana University Press: 1984).

4. See Kuno Fischer, *Hegels Leben, Werke, Lehre*, (Heidelberg, 1901) I, 506-7. See also Hegel, *Briefe*, I, 506-7, note by Hoffmeister.

5. *Briefe*, I, 393, Letter of February 5, 1812; *Letters*, 261: "It is no mean feat in the first half year of one's marriage to write a thirty-sheet book of the most abstruse contents. But the injustice of the times! ["Injuria temporum!"] I am no academic [Akademicus]. I would have needed another year to put it in proper form, but I need the money to live."

6. *Briefe*, II, 272, letter of June 9, 1821; *Letters*, 470: "You know that, on the one hand, I am an anxious man and, on the other hand, I like tranquility."

7. The street of Berlin where Hegel lived, and which he enjoyed.

8. *Briefe*, III, 202; *Letters*, 663. See also *Briefe*, I, 422.

9. See G. Bianquis, *La vie quotidienne en Allemagne à l'époque romantique*, Paris, 1958, 253.

10. See *Briefe*, II, 113-4 and p. 197; *Letters*, 413 and 333.

11. See the letter to Altenstein of May 16, 1829, *Briefe*, III, 256; *Letters*, 396f.

12. See, for example, *Briefe*, III, 256 and 258; *Letters*, 396f.

13. L. Geiger, *Berlin, 1688-1840* (Berlin, 1895) 588.

14. K. Hegel, *Leben und Erinnerungen* (Leipzig, 1900) 32.

II

The Family

Hegel's family life offered him good cause for anxiety as well. Fortunately he found much comfort in the affection of a beloved wife, and in the health of his two legitimate sons.

But as if to make him pay dearly for this bit of happiness, he suffered a great deal of domestic turmoil from other sources.

His mistress at Jena, Johanna Burckhardt,* long the cause of anxious cares, died in 1817. She had not succeeded in thwarting his marriage with Marie von Tucher in 1811, but as long as she lived she was a constant source of worry and torment.

Hence Hegel felt only relief at her passing, as he confessed to his friend Frommann:

> This death affected Ludwig more than me. My heart had long ago finished with her. I could still only fear unpleasant contacts between her and Ludwig—and thus indirectly with my wife—and extreme unpleasantness for myself.[1]

But with Johanna Burckhardt out of the picture, there remained Hegel's illegitimate son, Ludwig Fischer. The relations of the philosopher and his wife with him as child and young man consisted of an uninterrupted series of strains, conflicts and crises.

Perhaps less loved than the two legitimate children, he was frustrated, demanding and willful, an inveterate prankster. Ultimately he ran away, joined the Dutch army, and died in Batavia in 1831.

Hegel passed away two months later, not having heard of Ludwig's death.

In spite of all the precautions taken to hide the origins of this child, his presence in Berlin placed Hegel somewhat on the fringe of the — quite malicious — Berlin "polite society".

As if the son were not enough, there was also the philosopher's sister, Christiane Hegel! Had she read in the *Phenomenology* that a sister is irreplaceable? A repressed Antigone, she could not console herself with being able to bury her brother...

A spinster, she took offense on seeing him marry. She suffered from a morbid jealousy. The philosopher tried to appease her. He received her into his home, wrote her thoughtful letters, and helped her financially. But it was to no avail. She found fault and became more and more angry.

It was necessary to send her away, to look after her, and to watch out for her. She committed suicide in 1832 by drowning herself in the Nagold at Bad Teinach.

Hegel's life was poisoned by unfortunates who looked for death and took too long to find it. It was soured by the premature death of the friendships on which he counted the most.

Stäudlin committed suicide — people often committed suicide around Hegel. Sinclair died suddenly. Hölderlin, divorced from the life of the mind, became an incurable madman. Schelling forgot the fraternal ties of years before.

To be sure the worthy Niethammer remained, but his friendship was not of the same ilk. Hegel was never really on intimate terms with him. In Berlin Hegel benefited from prestigious patronage; he maintained friendly relations with colleagues, writers, scholars, artists and students. But outside of his sister and his wife, he addressed no one in familiar terms.

Not only did he enjoy no "omnipotence", nor bask in a continual "triumph"; on the contrary, he knew daily anguish. For this man it was not resignation that was necessary, but the courage to "recognize the rose in the cross of the present."[2] *

Professional, financial and family ties limited severely his freedom to manoeuvre in the political arena. Greater boldness would inevitably lead to dismissal and ruin. He could expect no friendly or helpful welcome in any other country. He could count on no support. Even scattered former students, like van

Ghert, who had offered to help him in possible difficulty, did not long retain power.[3]

Hegel was no hero. Yet is it not excessively severe to stigmatize his "cowardice"?[4]

He found himself without refuge and without help, alone, abandoned to the good pleasure of his employers and protectors. Others around him who would have been able to adopt an attitude of opposition and expose themselves to less risk, still refrained from doing so.

We shall see Hegel, vulnerable and afraid, push the limits that circumstance allowed; we shall see him nudge the breaking point.

NOTES

1. *Briefe*, II, 155; *Letters*, 434.

2. *Hegel's Philosophy of Right*, tr. T.M. Knox (Oxford, 1942) 12.

3. In 1830 van Ghert was ousted by his opponents.

4. W.R. Beyer, *Zwischen Phänomenologie und Logik. Hegel als Redakteur der Bamberger Zeitung* (Frankfurt a.M., 1955).

III

The Political Setting

1. Prussia

Throughout his long and hard quest for a secure position, in each of his successive relocations, Hegel followed the itinerary of a free spirit in Germany, each time attempting to settle in a country that promised to carry forward the interests of culture, political progress, and German patriotism.

During his stay in Switzerland, that country symbolized the ideal of freedom for many European intellectuals: though he strove to dispel that illusion in light of his experience. In Frankfurt he found a commercial and political metropolis allied with the initiative of the Confederation of the Rhine. When he went to Jena, that town, along with Weimar, had, under the aegis of the Duke of Saxe-Weimar and his minister, Goethe, become a centre of vigorous intellectual activity and heterodox thought. Hegel settled in Bavaria after the return of Montgelas to the direction of public affairs had opened a new era of progress, of active struggle against "superstition", and of the spread of new ideas.

And when he finally responded to the invitation of Altenstein, Prussia differed quite noticably from what it had been during his youth, when he had criticized it severely:

> But the kind of life and the barrenness that prevails in another state so regimented, namely the Prussian, strikes anyone who enters the first village, or who does not judge its strength by the ephemeral energy which a singular genius has been able to force upon it for a while.[1]

Prussia had changed. After 1815 almost all cultured and patriotic Germans had turned their eyes toward that country as it grew stronger, progressed, and became more eminent. Other German states, indeed other European countries, stagnated or regressed. In central Europe, Prussia alone advanced toward modern life and toward influence.

To be sure it did not extricate itself from the after-effects of feudalism completely, or in one leap. It did not adopt the methods of the French revolutionaries of '93.

Nevertheless it knew a type of regeneration, and it could take pride in some reforms, timid and partial though they might be. Its admirers valued not what it was, but what it promised to become, the hopes to which it gave birth. There was talk of the granting of a constitution; the word "progress" did not immediately invoke brutal repression. Exemplary efforts were being made to organize public education.

When he turned his steps towards Prussia, Hegel was not going back to the past. No doubt extreme slowness and serious deficiences in execution somewhat discouraged the Prussians. But nobody thought that all hope of social and political emancipation was to be abandonned, particularly as long as Hardenberg officially held the reins of government in his hands.

From a military point of view Prussia had demonstrated its ability to recover in the battles of 1813 and 1815. Its population surpassed that of any of the other members of the German Confederation. In 1816 it had ten and a half million inhabitants, while the German portions of Austria had only nine and a half million, and the kingdom of Bavaria trailed far behind with its three and a half million subjects.

It was in Prussia that the population grew the fastest. In 1837 Prussia's population would be fourteen million against eleven million Austrians. In this country and its dependent territories the largest and most rapid industrial expansion took place. The Prussian middle classes became the managers of the German bourgeoisie.

A patriot of a realistic and objective mind would not have been ignorant of this state of affairs. What motive could there be to lead Hegel to reject the hopes that were being raised at Berlin?

If one suspects Hegel of adopting a Prussian chauvinism, one must beware lest one abandon oneself to the promptings of an anti-Prussian chauvinism. Like many other countries, Prussia has produced the best and the worst.

In any case it is wise to use only with great caution a regional, provincial or national label to designate a style of life or to classify an economic and political regime.

At the beginning of the nineteenth century, Prussia owed its growth and power to a set of complex conditions and to a series of events too numerous to recount here. It owed them as well to reforms that rejuvenated it after the defeat at Jena. The reformers were men like Stein,* Hardenberg and Scharnhorst* who were no more Prussian than Hegel, but who, inspired by a burning patriotism, had come together in Prussia because they sensed and knew that the destiny of the German nation would, for some time to come, be entrusted to this land.

In 1807 Stein, invited to lead the administration after Napoleon had demanded and obtained the dismissal of Hardenberg, promulgated the famous *October Edicts*: legal abolition of serfdom; for everyone the right of access to land ownership, previously reserved to nobles; the organization of a genuinely Prussian ministry, with a state chancellor at its head; institution of elected municipalities in the towns; and so on.

Hardenberg, returning to power in 1810, completed Stein's reforms: equality in taxation, industrial freedom, abolition of corporations, suppression of feudal tenure, an attempt to convene an assembly of leading men.

These various measures were implemented in a much too fragmentary way; overall the feudal lords knew how to ward off the threats that would be most serious. Yet even so, by their proclamation and their partial realization they changed the traditional Prussia into one of the most "progressive" states in Germany, if not in Europe.

Frederick William III did not exactly welcome all these innovations. But he trusted Hardenberg, and feared for his crown. As Friedrich Engels said:

It was this fear which led him to allow a party of half-and-half reformers to govern in his stead—Hardenberg, Stein, Schön, Scharnhorst, and so on—who introduced a more liberal organization

of municipalities, abolition of serfdom, commutation of feudal
services into rents or into a fixed sum of twenty-five years purchase,
and above all, the military organization, which gives the people a
tremendous power, and which some time or other will be used
against the government. They also 'prepared' for a constitution
which, however, has not yet seen the light of day.[2]

This is all the more noteworthy in that the social and
political transformations were accompanied by a significant
consolidation of the foundations of intellectual life. Having
become in the eyes of the whole world the land that symbolized
universal public education, Prussia offered a shining symbol of
its metamorphosis: the University of Berlin, created in 1810
according to the plans of Wilhelm von Humboldt, whose first
rector was Fichte.

These innovations, and in particular the last, won over the
German intellectuals. They saw the seeds of a systematic
development of their national culture – indeed of culture in
general – at last coming to fruition.

When in 1815 Niethammer wrote to his friend Hegel that
"fortunately culture no longer needs to seek asylum in
Bavaria,"[3] he clearly implied that it had now found a place at
Berlin. And this man, who had for years waged a difficult
struggle in Bavaria to secure the rights of the Protestant
minority and the spread of classical culture, was soon also
focusing on Prussia his hopes of personal security and his
expectations of success for his cherished cause.

In 1819 he proposed enrolling his son at the University of
Berlin, and speaking of the Prussian capital he confided to
Hegel:

> I only wish that I could send all of us there at the same time! ... I
> know that a minister like Altenstein could usefully employ me; and it
> would suffice, perhaps, if he only knew it...

And he added:

> And besides, what Prussia could and should become from the point
> of view of the Church, could not possibly lie in the hearts of very
> many people more than in mine.[4]

German Protestants generally considered Catholicism to be an ally of reaction. They prided themselves in representing better than the Catholics a kind of political liberalism, a greater openness to new ideas.

It is easy to grasp, then, what sort of hope could arise in Hegel's mind at the sight of the reforming activity in Prussia: the progressive liquidation of the feudal system, the solid establishment of a national pole of attraction, the spread of culture, and the defence of Protestantism understood as a religion of freedom opposed to Catholic "servitude" and "obscurantism".

No other country in Germany could legitimize such dreams.

This country now recognized Hegel's worth, and issued an invitation to him. For once Hegel triumphed over his traditional rival, Fries. This tardy vindication came about in an impressive way. His Excellency, the Minister of Public Education himself sought Hegel's consent.

To be sure, the cross of the present remained heavy to carry, but never had the little rose smelled so sweet!*

2. The Restoration

Why did the Prussian government invite Hegel rather than another philosopher?

The traditional response to this question is that Hegel was chosen to play the philosopher's role for the Prussian restoration. It had need of an ideological watchdog, charged not only with combatting liberal and revolutionary theories, but also with diverting the paths of groups of intellectuals away from them.

This opinion continues to be quite widespread. A. Stern, for example, lays it to Hegel's account in a recent article. While commenting on, and arbitrarily interpreting, Hegel's celebrated saying about "the owl of Minerva who spreads its wings only with the falling of dusk," he states:

> With these words the ultra-conservative Hegel wanted to deter the impetuous, youthful partisans of philosophical theories whose objective was to reform the policies of the Prussian monarchy. To

fulfil this task Hegel had been called to the University of Berlin in 1818 by the Prussian minister of education, von Altenstein.

Yet this author seems to contradict himself directly several lines further on when he notes, speaking of Hegel, that this "ultra-conservative" was

> a witness to the French Revolution which he admired as the supreme triumph of reason and of the idea of law in politics.[5]

Some biographers of Hegel, without claiming that Hegel came to Berlin expressly to support the reaction, nevertheless assert that he spontaneously adopted such a political attitude and that his own system of thought necessarily led him in that direction. Lucien Herr makes this argument in a well-known article in the *Grande Encyclopédie*:

> It is undeniable that his theory owed the triumphant speed of its reception to Prussia. It was the official and imposed doctrine, and he himself did not scruple in using the accomodating authority of the state against dissidents. But it is not quite correct to say that he placed his thought at the service of Prussian authoritarianism simply to be agreeable or submissive. In his eyes the authoritarian monarchy and bureaucracy of restored Prussia appeared to be, if not the perfect political regime, at least the regime best adapted to the political conceptions that resulted from his system.[6]

Yet quite clearly Hegel's philosophy as it was known *in 1818* did not lead to such conclusions. Indeed, these do not proceed necessarily even from the *Philosophy of Right* of 1821.

As for the politically confused notion of authoritarianism, it signifies the means used rather than the end intended, even though, as we well know, contamination can occur and bad means corrupt the best end. But the authoritarianism of the *Committee of Safety* was not reactionary, and Hardenberg probably never showed himself less conservative than on that courageous day when, without any form of trial, he locked up some Prussian Junkers hostile to his reforms in Spandau.[7]

Furthermore, does the king of Hegelian stamp whose function consists in "saying yes" and in "putting the dot on the *i*" have an authoritarian manner? In the *Philosophy of History*, Hegel spells out what real power he accords to this monarch:

The government rests with the official world, and the personal decision of the monarch constitutes its apex; for a final decision is, as was remarked above, absolutely necessary. Yet with firmly established laws, and a settled organization of the state, what is left to the sole arbitration of the monarch is, in point of substance, no great matter. It is certainly a very fortunate circumstance for a nation, when a sovereign of noble character falls to its lot, yet in a great state even this is of small moment, since its strength lies in the Reason incorporated in it.[8]

Hegel did not ratify the claims of the restoration. Neither Frederick William III nor (above all) Frederick William IV would have tolerated being reduced to simply writing a signature; they demonstrated in fact that their pretensions extended well beyond these narrow limits.

The Hegelian monarch had emerged from the great revolutionary convulsion quite crippled: the model had been profoundly transformed in 1789. Hegel never stopped admiring and appreciating the French Revolution.[9] He continued collecting documents on it and, on his trip to Paris, he visited and was moved by all of its key sites.

During the European restoration it was the thing to do to defame and anathematize the Revolution; the very justice of God had been revealed with a vengeance[10] in the course taken by the Revolution: God had used it to exact retribution.

Hegel grew angry when he heard such puerile condemnations of an event he considered to be, along with the Reformation, the most important in world history.

Read again the angry words he wrote in 1827 on reading a text in which Sir Walter Scott claimed that the French Revolution had been God's punishment for the sins of France and of Europe:

How is that? If the sins of France and of Europe were so great that a *just* God inflicted the most fearsome punishment on this part of the world, the revolution would then have been *necessary*; not a new crime, but rather retribution for crimes formerly committed. Pretentious words, which would scarcely be pardoned coming from a Capuchin who wanted to disguise his ignorance. It also appears that just as unknown to him are the characteristic principles that identify the essence of the Revolution and that give it its almost immeasurable power over the mind.

And referring to Walter Scott, who accused "the most spiritual people in Europe" of letting themselves "be seduced by the coarsest illusions and the most perverse principles" Hegel could not resist the exclamation: "Dunce!"[11]

Is it not significant that, barely a year after the *Philosophy of Right* appeared, Hegel went to see Lazare Carnot* in the citadel of Magdeburg, his compulsory residence? The French and Prussian monarchists and their respective police maintained a particular surveillance over this exile, who was suspected of preparing, even then, for a revolutionary movement in France. Hardenberg had certainly given evidence of his respect for the unfortunate republican, but he could not spare him all the consequences of the animosity of the French "ultras", worried about the mysterious activities of Carnot in Germany.[12]

In a letter to his wife, Hegel spoke in moving terms about the political personality with whom he had just spoken, who symbolized everything that the restoration abhorred and repudiated: the regicide, the organizer of revolutionary victory, and the faithful republican:

> But of all that I saw the most treasured sight was General Carnot, a kind old man and a Frenchman. It was the famous Carnot; he took it kindly that I looked him up.[13]

For if Napoleon, in the process of ensuring some of his conquests, had stabilized and arrested the bourgeois revolution in France, he had also extended it to all Europe.

> Napoleon (notes Engels) was in Germany the representative of the revolution, the propagator of its principles, the destroyer of the old feudal society.... Napoleon applied the *reign of terror*, which had done its work in France, *to other countries in the shape of war* — and this "reign of terror" was sadly wanted in Germany.[14]

In Napoleon European aristocrats indeed discerned their enemy; they compared the "Corsican monster" to the Jacobins; they hated him as much as Robespierre. As Ancillon wrote in

1816: "In him the Revolution is personified."[15] From that pen such a declaration was certainly not intended to be praise!

Over the years, the revolutionary character of the Napoleonic empire was watered down somewhat; Napoleon's ascendency over Europe, socially progressive though it was, showed itself more and more to be oppressive for the nationalities. Nonetheless, Hegel experienced regret when Napoleon was finally defeated.

And when the restoration began to exact its revenge on Europe what sentiments did our philosopher feel?

We have to stress that all his previous political thought and all his philosophical work was fundamentally and irreducibly opposed even to the principle of a restoration. Moreover, Hegel's logic was not content with condemning a return to the past; it challenged the very possibility of a simple permanence of thought and of human institutions; so it rejected conservatism.

In Hegel's philosophy, restoration as a real possibility is excluded from history by his doctrine of the irreversibility of the course of events. Hegel abhorred all revivals and imitations, always superficial and fraudulent, and abhorred as well the simulation or mimicking of a revival, even in details or appearance. He upbraided the French revolutionaries for having now and again aped the Romans of antiquity in their language and clothes.*

Yet the idea of *restoration* in politics implies the full re-establishment of a former type of government, the return to a former regime, the recall of a dynasty previously ousted.

Hegel did accept repetition – at least an approximation of it – only in several domains of the real world: mechanics, and also biology. Thus, for example, in animals the constant law of species implies a resemblance in successive individual existences. To illustrate this cyclical movement, this eternal return, Hegel puts forward the image of the phoenix which is born again incessantly from its ashes, and he deplores its monotony.[16]

But the life of the spirit escapes this tedium; it stimulates continual progress:

The rejuvenation of spirit is not a bare return to the same form; it is a purifying, a reworking of itself. In achieving its task, it creates for itself new tasks by which it multiplies the raw material for its labour. Thus we see in history the spirit issue forth in an inexhaustible multitude of directions, enjoy itself and find satisfaction in them. But its labour has still only the one result, to multiply its activity once again and to consume itself once again. It continually encounters each of its creations, in which it has found satisfaction, as new raw material which demands of it a new reworking. What is its culture becomes the material which its labour uses to elevate it to a new culture.[17]

Now it is in history that spirit really reigns. Less than anywhere else could Hegel here allow a relapse into an out-of-date phase. A political restoration, brought about by men "who have learned nothing and forgotten nothing," appeared to him, strictly speaking, impossible.

Van Ghert clearly expressed the same thought as his master when he wrote to him in 1817:

It seems that everywhere they want to return to the middle ages, which is, however, impossible, for the spirit of the times has made too much progress to be able to retreat. How can one will the impossible?[18]

Spirit is by definition that which always advances. An actual reaction would represent the death of spirit, a fall into bestiality or mechanism, a victory of the inhuman.

As an historical event, then, the restoration did not entirely deserve its name according to Hegel. It was merely an *attempt* at restoration, fatally unproductive.

Reactionaries *think themselves* to be re-establishing the former social and political relations. In reality they render themselves guilty of an operation even more pernicious, and at the same time ridiculous.

They introduce a regime that tries to resemble the past without succeeding, and that certainly revives some of the faults of the former regime, now aggravated because of their anachronism and because of the wide-spread sense of their decrepitude. In the new conditions that the age places on them, they fall lower than their models; they augment the despotism that they try to imitate; they render the arbitrary more capricious and the obscure even more cloudy; they surpass the limits of ridicule.

What they achieve lacks truth because the result of their manoeuvres does not correspond to the concept of what they are pursuing. Their work (is that an appropriate word?) is marked especially by its lack of self-awareness and its hypocrisy. It embodies the illusion of attributing the value of everything which has just emerged in the present and which remains irrevocably in place to the past.

This illusion never lasts for long. The dilapidated structures are replastered, but the spirit that built them cannot be revived. Spiritual ruins never rise again.

3. The Giant of Progress

So Hegel was opposed in principle to a restoration. In practice, however, he could have forgotten the demands of his theory. In practice too, the restoration — disowning its name and declared intentions — could have accomplished a worthwhile political task, followed the spirit of the times, created beneficial institutions and introduced a new style of life.

In fact the restoration in Europe showed itself to be as bad in its acts as in its designs, and Hegel abhorred it in practice as much as he condemned it in theory.

He did not rejoice in the fall of Napoleon; quite the contrary. Fascinated by the destiny of the great man, he even seems to have remained unaware of the political significance and the historical importance of the Prussian people's uprising against the foreign occupier in 1813 and 1815.

He spent that period in Bavaria, where he had lived since the battle of Jena. From there the defeat of Napoleon presented most obviously the picture of reaction's victory and revenge. His friends in Berlin, and in particular the heroic combatant, Friedrich Förster, later told him what the patriotic reflex was in Prussia; they doubtless pointed out its popular and anti-aristocratic character.

But in 1814 in Bavaria Hegel could not consider without bitterness the possibility of a return to the former conditions of political life; hence he showed his hostility to Prussia and its allies.[19]

Hegel watched all his political hopes evaporate at the same time that the domination of "Paris's great teacher of law", Napoleon, came to an end. The philosopher commented on that defeat in this way:

> There is nothing more *tragic* (Hegel uses the Greek: *tragikotaton*). The entire mass of mediocrity, with its irresistible leaden weight of gravity, presses on, without rest or reconciliation, until it has succeeded in bringing down what is high to the same level or even below.[20]

That is how Hegel assessed the conquerors of Napoleon, the knights of the Holy Alliance, the Tsar and Metternich, the German princes and the king of Prussia: *mediocrity*.

Niethammer and he shared their anxiety and their bitterness with each other. Hegel's friend was already imagining the restoration giving the coup-de-grâce to his fragile plan for the organization of public education in Bavaria; and he regarded the threats that menaced him personally and those which weighed on all of Europe with the same contempt. Here is the picture of reaction triumphant as he sketched it for Hegel:

> Just as worms, frogs and other vermin often follow the rain, so the Weillers and their ilk follow the dark day now spreading out over the entire civilized world. In this universal flood -- the wages of sin -- in which all that has been cast aside returns, this literary and pedagogical rabble, following the example of all other rabbles, believes it has finally found its hour; and, I begin to fear, has indeed found it![21]

The restoration: a deluge thanks to which the out-of-date takes the place of the new — and all sorts of scoundrels profit from the substitution.

Immediately Hegel replied to Niethammer:

> This colorless, tasteless intermediary state, which allows nothing to get too bad and nothing too good, for once rules our world.

And, faced with this vista, he passed through a moment of discouragement and disgust; he shall concern himself with nothing more than the details of his personal affairs, with his salary. He refused to continue

to take all that much to heart further interests in the matter, nor interests in honour, even if it still takes these interests in hand and — insofar as it is necessary and possible — in head.[22]

In the disarray of political hopes, personal self-centredness acquires for a moment the upper hand. But not for long!

By June 1816 Niethammer will vilify "this tumult of fools and simpletons", and "the weakness which holds the reins and behaves in a ridiculous way"; he will gravely proclaim his faith in the direction of history:

The peoples today struggle for political liberty just as three hundred years ago they struggled for religious liberty; and the princes, blinded almost in the same way as then to the breach that has already occurred, try to set up dikes to counter the impetuous flood.

One can appreciate why "for this communication" as he calls it, he had judged it preferable not to use "the official and public post", but rather the good services of the "private and closed post" of travelling theological students.[23]

It is certainly by means of the same "private post", sheltered from the curiosity of the police, that Hegel forwarded to Niethammer his remarkable letter of July 5, 1816, which detailed his attitude with regard to the Restoration.

It is no longer a question for Hegel of limiting himself to the confines of his personal interests. On the contrary:

More general events and expectations in the world at large, just as in more immediate circles, move me most of all to increasingly general considerations, which push particular details and immediate happenings further aside in my thoughts, however much these hold interest for feeling.[24]

And he expounds for his friend a kind of political creed:

I adhere to the view that the world spirit has given the age marching orders. These orders are being obeyed. The world spirit, this essential [power], proceeds irresistibly like a closely drawn armored phalanx advancing with imperceptible movement, much as the sun through thick and thin.

And he appeals to the "advancing giant" whose impetus cannot be slowed by the mindless struggles that break out around it. The giant has at its command rubber soles; it wears "seven-league boots"; we have to keep our eyes on it without worrying about the innumerable obstacles that are thrown up to stop it. To amuse ourselves, we can even pretend to support the efforts of those who wish to hold it back; nothing will stop it.

Perhaps Hegel underestimates the powers of the reactionaries—the uncomprehending dwarfs—too much; doubtless he trusts too much in the spontaneity of historical movement—the giant who always progresses through thick and thin. Nevertheless he does not leave any doubt about which side he opts for:

> I have anticipated the Reaction of which we presently hear so much. It wishes to impose its right. "*La vérité en la repoussant, on l'embrace*" [while repudiating the truth, one embraces it] as a deep saying of Jacobi's goes. The Reaction is still far removed from genuine resistance; ... Even if it intends to do the opposite, its will of the Reaction is chiefly restricted to matters of vanity. It wishes to place its own stamp on the events it thinks it most vehemently hates, so as to read upon them: 'This we have done!'

It will change little more than appearances. As to any real damage that it introduces, Hegel does not believe it to be lasting:

> For when such injury pretends to a more significant relation to the whole substance than it is capable of having, it proves ephemeral.[25]

Later, Hegel would learn to fear the real powers of reaction. For the moment, at the end of the month of July, 1816, he felt a contemptuous hostility for them. At the beginning of August, his name was considered by Berlin for the first time. Did they really hope to make him the official philosopher of the restoration? Did they believe him capable of pronouncing a philosophic panegyric of the resurrected past?

When Hegel experienced nostalgia, his dreams did not take him to the Middle Ages, to absolute monarchy, or to the Holy Roman Empire. If there were a question of returning to the past, he ventured to plunge much further. He preferred to recall the enchantment of the ancient Greek republics – forever lost, to be sure, but always lamented.

Whatever might be the excesses of his theory of historical spontaneity and the inadequacies of his view of the origins of events, one thing remains certain: he did not hope for the return of the "good old days" at all.[26] And he resolutely condemned the diplomatic duplicity, the sorry carving up of the European nations which the victors of 1815 became involved in. With reference to the negotiations at Vienna, he wrote:

> The common predicate 'deficient' must undoubtedly be attributed to their progress. It is a new, unforgettable experience for the people to see what their Princes are capable of when they convene to devote themselves in mind and heart to discussion of the welfare of both their own peoples and the world – all, to be sure, according to the most nobly declared principle of universal justice and the welfare of all. ... The present phenomenon ... is unique and calls for a brilliant result.[27]

A complementary motif increased Hegel's disaffection with the restoration still more: the spread and revival of the power of Catholicism. In Bavaria the problem of religious freedom assumed decisive importance for the Protestants. Hegel did not watch Catholicism reconquer men, institutions and countries without anxiety.

He shared with Niethammer unhappy news (which would later prove to be false), concerning the misfortune of their mutual friend, the naturalist Schubert, who had just left Bavaria, finding it too Catholic and too reactionary for his taste:

> Schubert has found a nice mess in Ludwigslust. Upon his arrival he found the hereditary Grand Duke, along with the entire court of hangers-on, converted to Catholicism. Another sign of the times.[28]

In his reply to Hegel, who also wanted to leave Bavaria, Niethammer expressed the hope that he not find elsewhere "an improvement as at Ludwigslust."[29]

Perhaps at this period of his life in particular Hegel seemed to attach himself to Protestantism as an antidote to Catholicism. Discretely in public, more openly in private, he always presented it under its least sectarian and most liberal aspect: a religion of freedom.

On this point he remained true to the ideas he had expressed to Niethammer as early as 1810:

> Protestantism does not so much consist in any special creed as in the spirit of reflection and higher rational education, not in the spirit of drill serving this or that utilitarian purpose.[30]

He reaffirmed this opinion in 1816:

> Protestantism is not entrusted to the hierarchical organization of a Church but lies solely in general insight and culture. ... Our universities and schools are our church.[31]

These religious views can hardly be said to sin by an excess of conformity or orthodoxy when compared with the dogmas of confessional statements. But to appreciate their real audacity we have to place them as well in their historical context. In the Prussia of 1821 a royal edict proscribed the use of the words 'Protestant, Protestantism'; they were judged to be too ambiguous, and to evoke revolutionary echoes. The censors were asked to substitute the words 'Evangelical, Evangelicalism' for them.[32]

This, then, is the way Hegel's thought was related to "authoritarian monarchism" around 1815. We search in vain for his supposed taste for reaction, his respect for sovereigns, his submission to orthodoxy.

Did Hegel maintain his political choices of 1815 and 1816 in later years? Did he not come to terms with absolutism at the time of his nomination to Berlin in 1818?

Let us rest assured: never did Hegel bind the fate of his theories to the success of the reaction; never did he become the bard of the restoration.[33] Others aspired to provide a 'philosophy' for the restoration. He criticized them, attacking them by name, in his *Philosophy of Right*.

Would he have been, then, a secretive or unsuspecting conformist? Why do some authors persist in seeing him as a "thinker of the restoration"?[34]

To us this obstinacy seems to result from an equally persistent oversight: ignoring the actual political conditions in which Hegel lived at Berlin.

We are in Prussia. In this land and its capital the "Jacobins of 1793" never held power, nor did the moderates of 1791, nor, indeed, the indecisive bystanders of those days. Here the monarchy has never really been questioned.

To be sure, Napoleon struck several strong blows against it, which served to make it shudder, but the whole Prussian nation was affected as well.

To what, then, would a *restoration*, in the proper sense of the term, apply? There is nothing to restore since nothing has been destroyed. The Prussian Junkers certainly backed the *European* movement of restoration and took part in it. They supported the Holy Alliance.

But in Prussia it was less a matter of returning to a previous hegemony than of meeting head on the *contemporary* attempts at reform. "To restore" was to be more obstinate in maintaining what the population passively accepted.³⁵

The Junkers considered "revolutionaries" not only the Montagnards, but also the Girondins, the Feuillants, the partisans of Napoleon, the subjects who demanded a constitution, the enlightenment philosophers, and the admirers of Frederick II!*

They hated the *Code civil* as much as the *Constitution* of 1793; the idea of a constitution in general as much as the idea of a republic.

It is possible that Hegel did not much like the Jacobins of 1793. That has been claimed. But it is certain that he followed for some time the Girondins; he admired the *Code civil* and constitutional government. The right to property appeared to him an irreversible achievement.

What triumphs the French Revolution had achieved—bourgeois rights—he wanted to preserve, or alternatively to have introduced. And he said so in the *Philosophy of Right* in words more or less veiled. For we cannot forget the conditions in which he published this work. In fact it is quite remarkable that it was allowed to appear at all.³⁶ We owe that in part to the protection in high places from which Hegel benefited, and also in part to the skill of the author, who knew how to render his words obscure for the censors, at the risk, to be sure, of misleading his friends about their actual meaning.

Hegel knew what was involved in the relations between philosophy and the authorities. "The latter," he said, "tolerate philosophy only when it is completely inoffensive."

His own was not entirely so; we will see that soon enough. But in that case we are faced with the question: Why did they then turn to Hegel if they did not expect him to teach a philosophy of the restoration?

NOTES

1. "The Constitution of Germany," in Carl J. Friedrich, *The Philosophy of Hegel* (New York, 1954) 537.

2. F. Engels, "The State of Germany," Letter II, November 8, 1845, in Marx-Engels *Collected Works* (New York, 1967) VI, 23.

3. *Briefe*, II, 59.

4. *Briefe*, II, 208-9. See *Letters*, 440f.

5. A. Stern, "L'Irréversibilité de l'Histoire," *Diogène*, Paris, xxix, 4.

6. *Grande Encyclopédie*, xix, 998.

7. See F. Mehring, *Historische Aufsätze zur preussisch-deutschen Geschichte* (Berlin, 1952) 221.

8. G.W.F. Hegel, *The Philosophy of History*, tr. Sibree (New York, 1956) 456. Hegel confirmed this opinion in the *Lectures on Aesthetics*: "So too, monarchs in our day, unlike the heroes of the mythical ages, are no longer the concrete heads of the whole, but a more or less abstract centre of institutions already independently developed and established by law and the constitution. The most important acts of government the monarchs of our time have renounced; they no longer pronounce judgement themselves; finance, civil organization and security is no longer their special business; war and peace are determined by general international relations which no longer are within their single power or conducted by them as individuals. And even if in all these matters the final, supreme decision is theirs, still what is really decreed is not so much a matter of their personal will; it has already been settled independently, so that the supremacy of the monarch's own subjective will in

respect of universal and public affairs is only of a formal kind." *Hegel's Aesthetics*, tr. Knox (Oxford, 1975) I, 193-4.

9. See J.Hyppolite, "The Significance of the French Revolution in Hegel's Phenomenology," in *Studies in Marx and Hegel*, tr. O'Neill (New York, 1969) 35-69.

10. See F. Ancillon, *Ueber Souveränität und Staatsverfassungen* (Berlin, 1816) 76.

11. G.W.F. Hegel, *Berliner Schriften*, ed. Hoffmeister (Hamburg, 1956) 658.

12. See M. Reinhard, *Le grand Carnot* (Paris, 1952) II, 331-32.

13. *Briefe*, II, 340; *Letters*, 580.

14. Engels, "The State of Germany," 1st letter, in Marx-Engels *Collected Works*, VI, 19.

15. Ancillon, *Ueber Souveränität* ..., 34.

16. G.W.F. Hegel, *Vorlesungen über die Philosophie der Weltgeschichte*, Bd. I, *Die Vernunft in der Geschichte* (Hamburg, 1958) 35. (This version of the introduction to the *Philosophy of History* has not yet been translated into English.)

17. Ibid, 35-36.

18. *Briefe*, II, 159.

19. See the letter to Niethammer of April 29, 1814. *Briefe*, II, 27; *Letters*, 306f.

20. *Briefe*, II, 28; *Letters*, 307.

21. *Briefe*, II, 59; *Letters*, 319.

22. *Briefe*, II, 61; *Letters*, 320.

23. *Briefe*, II, 85; *Letters*, 324. This final comment in Niethammer's letter, which reveals the precautions taken by the two friends to protect the privacy of their correspondence, is not reproduced by K. Hegel in the first incomplete edition of Hegel's correspondence. See *Briefe von und an Hegel*, ed. K. Hegel (Berlin, 1887) 400. It is also not included in the English edition.

24. *Briefe*, II, 85; *Letters*, 325.

25. *Briefe*, II, 85-86; *Letters*, 325.

26. See *Briefe*, II, 27; *Letters*, 307.

27. *Briefe*, II, 47; *Letters*, 313f.

28. *Briefe*, II, 79; *Letters*, 323.

29. *Briefe*, II, 79.

30. *Briefe*, I, 337; *Letters*, 227.

31. *Briefe*, II, 89; *Letters*, 327.

32. See F. Schnabel, *Deutsche Geschichte im neunzehnten Jahrhundert (Freiburg, 1949) II, 261.*

33. Even though B. Croce affirms: "Politically Hegel was a conservative and in some respects even a reactionary." *Revue de métaphysique et de morale,* 1931, 284.

34. E. Bloch, *Subjekt-Objekt* (Berlin, 1952) 34.

35. In the *Introduction to the Critique of Hegel's Philosophy of Law,* (1844) Marx wrote: "For we shared the restoration of the modern nations although we had not shared their revolutions. We underwent a restoration first because other nations dared to carry out a revolution and second because other nations suffered a counter-revolution." Marx-Engels, *Collected Works,* (New York, 1975) III, 176.

36. The application of the edict of censorship, promulgated in October 18, 1819 in Prussia, delayed for a year the appearance of the *Principles of the Philosophy of Right (Briefe,* II, 447, note 1).

IV

Patrons

1. The Nomination to Berlin

Hegel's nomination to Berlin marked the end of a series of initiatives and negotiations, whose ups and downs followed one another over several years.

A first attempt in 1816 miscarried. The second one, in 1818, was successful.

The Prussian capital had attracted Hegel for some time. He wanted to live "at the centre", as he said, particularly in order to follow developments in political and social life more closely. He had himself looked for some way of getting there.

The nature of the people he canvassed reveals clearly enough that he was in no way concerned to become the theoretician of the reaction. He first turned to his friend Sinclair,[1] then in 1814 to Paulus,* and finally to Niethammer.

None of these men could pass for time-servers. Quite the contrary. And that, moreover, serves to explain in part the lack of success of their initiatives.

Niethammer undertook official soundings without apparent result. Solger later prided himself in having been the first, in 1816, to propose Hegel officially for the chair left vacant by the death of Fichte.

The Minister of National Education, Von Schuckmann, whose politics were quite obscurantist at the time, gathered information on Hegel, invited reports from Raumer and Niebuhr* on the question, and allowed matters to drag out too long.

When he finally decided, Hegel had just accepted a position at Heidelberg.

Do not be misled! Schuckmann would have conducted the affair more openly, and Hegel would have quickly been installed at Berlin if the Hegelian philosophy had been of a sufficiently conservative character. Its reputation of "obscurity" was not the only thing that motivated the minister's hesitation.

In 1818 Schuckmann was replaced by Altenstein. The new "Minister of Public Education, of Religion and of Health" took a trip to Munich. There he visited Jacobi, who sang the praises of Hegel, his friend at the time, and who warmly recommended him to the minister.

In this case it was in no way a question of reactionary caution. In Bavaria Jacobi was considered—with what exaggeration—as a "Jacobin", an Enlightenment man and a heretic, and he was subjected to all sorts of attacks, some of them violent, from the Bavarian "ultras".[2]

Later, Hegel did not hide what he owed to Jacobi, whose political attitude was not unknown to him. In August 1818 he wrote a letter in French to Victor Cousin, who was then preparing to make a trip to Munich, and he had this to say:

> I enclose a letter for Mr. Roth, Councillor at the Ministry of Finance, a financial expert but above all a historian and political scientist. He occupies the same house as Mr. Jacobi, to whom I ask him to present you, and to whom even without such a presentation you would not fail to pay a visit. Please show him all the respect and affection I never cease to feel for him, and tell him likewise that I have not forgotten that it was he who gave the first impetus to my call to Berlin. ... You will find these gentlemen very liberal in their way of thinking, though with nuances you will easily grasp and which perhaps tend a bit toward this Teutonic, anti-French patriotism.[3]

Can anyone conclude that Hegel owed his nomination to Berlin to his retrograde ideas? They are perhaps thinking of the *Principles of the Philosophy of Right*. These certainly do not deserve such a bad reputation,[4] and in any case they could not have influenced his nomination, which was decided three years before they appeared. Perhaps they show the effects of having breathed the air of Berlin. But they could not have provided a guarantee of Hegel's politics.

If Prussia had wanted to find a partisan of absolutism to place at its service, would it have gone to look in Bavaria, among the enlightenment figures that Montgelas, in the period of his omnipotence, had gathered to this land? Would it have chosen a friend of Sinclair, Paulus, Thiersch, Goethe, Knebel, and Niethammer?

But are we not giving a false picture of Prussia in 1818, and of the Prussian leaders, when we qualify them globally and indifferently as behind the times? In the only European country which at the time offered the luxury of some reforms, albeit timid, it would be paradoxical if we could not discover some men of progress.

We will meet them in proximity to Hegel if we are willing to examine the philosopher's relations with each of the principal holders of power and with each of the important segments of opinion.

2. Hardenberg

In 1818 Prince von Hardenberg was head of the Prussian government, and he continued there until his death four years later. At 70 years of age he was putting the finishing touches to a life that revealed his great faults—frivolity and dissipation—but also his great virtues: cleverness, intelligence, and patriotism.

In the course of his long career he had on occasion given way to the pressures of reaction. He could thus be accused of having sometimes lacked tenacity, although one should remember that most of the time his adversaries had at their command more powerful forces.

Sometimes kept at bay, sometimes triumphant, the feudal lords were none the less his enemies. He belonged to the other camp. When Hegel later sent him a complimentary copy of his *Philosophy of Right*, he did not fail to mention the "enlightened government" [erleuchtete Regierung] of Prince von Hardenberg, and these words assumed a special significance when everything associated with "enlightenment", with the *Aufklärung* and with "Illuminism" was suspect and even prosecuted.[5]

Would it have been possible, however, to characterize Hardenberg in any better way? He was an "enlightened" man, in the 18th century sense of the word .

In his youth he quickly made clear his sympathies for the *Aufklärung* and his inclination to scepticism. After a period of diplomatic apprenticeship in the service of the state of Hannover, which he had to leave for reasons pertaining to his private life, he placed himself in 1782 at the disposition of Brunswick, one of the most progressive German states of the time.

At the Brunswick court of those days there resided several refugee intellectuals, happy in finding there a despotism more tolerable than elsewhere. One of them was the educator Campe, with whom Hardenberg developed a plan for the reform of public instruction, inspired by Pestalozzi, which proposed the separation of the schools from religious control so that young minds would be prepared for the struggle against orthodoxy.

The clergy and nobility easily prevented the adoption of the Campe-Hardenberg plan. But the idea of a transformation of political life and of the state through a preliminary reform of education would henceforth be associated with Hardenberg. He would always favour the progress of public education; and he would later support the efforts of his friends to provide for Prussia an exemplary school organization, one whose existence and continual improvements Hegel would vouch for.

When his private life provoked another scandal, Hardenberg soon found himself dismissed by the Duke of Brunswick, and he entered the employ of Prussia in 1792.

In subordinate positions at the beginning of his career in this country, he gave an indication of his hostility to the feudal system and to restrictive traditions, and of his preference for a modern state, conducive to the development of culture and general welfare.

He quickly scaled the levels of the administrative and political hierarchy. In 1807 he became Prime Minister, but soon, on the order of Napoleon, the king of Prussia removed him from power and forced him to emigrate.

Together with other Prussian patriots, Hardenberg then took refuge at Riga. While there, he drafted with Altenstein and Niebuhr the famous *Treatise to the King* on the reorganization of the state, in which were expressed the main themes of his political thought.

Let us select several passages which will serve to show its spirit. Von Hardenberg noted that the events of the past years served to

> destroy everywhere what is weak, powerless and out of date and, following a path like the one nature takes in the physical world, to give new life to forces promoting progress towards perfection.

Von Hardenberg's *Treatise* includes an impassioned plea for "the spirit of the times" and for necessary reforms:

> The state which is successful in grasping the true spirit of the time and through the wisdom of its government working quietly and without the need of violent convulsions within that world scheme has undoubtedly a great advantage and its members must bless the care and concern that works so beneficially on their behalf.

Where does Hardenberg find the example of such progress? He provides an answer himself:

> The French Revolution, which the present wars are continuing, and with all its bloodletting and storms, gave the French a completely new direction. All the dormant forces were awakened; destroyed were misery and weakness, antiquated prejudices and crimes, together, to be sure, with much that was good.

In 1807 he condemned in advance all attempts at restoration:

> The illusion that one can resist the revolution most surely by holding fast to the old and by vigorously persecuting the principles that hold sway in such times has in fact resulted in producing the revolution and in giving it a steadily expanding influence. The authority of those principles is so great, they are so generally acknowledged and promulgated, that the state that does not adopt them shall be faced either with accepting them forcibly, or with its own downfall.

This is the way Prince von Hardenberg sums up the political program that he proposes to Prussia and its king:

> Thus a revolution in the good sense, leading directly to the great goal of ennobling mankind through the wisdom of government and not through violent forces coming from inside or out – that is our goal,

our governing principle. Democratic principles within a monarchy, such appears to me to be the form appropriate to the spirit of our present times.[6]

The individual proposals of the treatise of Riga suggested instituting a national representative assembly in Prussia, took issue with the privileges of the nobility, and demanded economic and political freedom.

Soon recalled to government, Hardenberg gave proof of his patriotism and on occasion of his courage. He constantly endeavoured to get a little democracy introduced into Prussian political life. Never did he disown his project for a national representative assembly; he struggled against the Prussian feudal lords, the Junkers and the courtiers, on occasion ruthlessly.

But overall the feudal party showed itself the stronger. Prussian feudalism succeeded in circumventing the regulations, in countering the main blows, and in maintaining itself. Towards the end the king sided more and more decisively with the nobles and the reaction. When Hardenberg died, the tension between him and the court had become intense.

He certainly was no Jacobin, yet the reaction condemned him as one. He certainly was no precursor of socialism. But because he tried unsuccessfully to bring about agrarian reform, the Junkers called him a "Leveller". He embodied the middle class reform movement in the Prussia of his time; he exhibited its good intentions, as well as all of its weaknesses.[7]

Cavaignac sketches a sympathetic portrait of the reforming Chancellor:

Hardenberg personified to some extent the influence of the French Revolution on the only German people who had undertaken social reform on their own, who had not received it completely from the hands of France.[8]

He notes that the German historians do not always do justice to Hardenberg's reforms and ideas, or to his politics in general, because they find there, to their dismay, the influence of the French Revolution. By and large they prefer Stein and even Schön* to him.

But (says Cavaignac) Hardenberg towers over them in the breadth of
his conceptions and the loftiness of view with which he developed his
guiding principles. Not only did he in 1811 anticipate both Stein and
Schön; not only did he, using political skill of the first order, know
how to introduce into the Prussian government a new politics and to
guide the king's will towards it; not only did he ensure the entrée into
public affairs of the only man who could succeed him;... but he alone
knew from the beginning how to discern clearly and expound
precisely and with singular nobility the general principles that should
govern what he called the regeneration of the Prussian state; these
principles were indeed those of the French Revolution.[9]

The assessment of Hardenberg made by the Marxist
historians is less enthusiastic, and lays greater stress on his
weakness in not accomplishing his good intentions; yet it does
not fundamentally contradict the opinion of Cavaignac. This is
how Franz Mehring characterizes the work of Hardenberg:

Like Stein he was not a Prussian by birth and possessed a certain
amount of bourgeois culture; indeed more than Stein he could be
called a liberal in the modern sense of the word. Superficial and
malleable, he simply copied the model of the kingdom of Westphalia
in the second period of bourgeois reform now beginning. ...
Hardenberg too was a thorn in the flesh of the Junkers; indeed he
had once sent some of their leaders to Spandau prison without trial
or law. Yet they preferred to stick with him since, even with his
liberal style, he understood all the same how to conduct their
affairs.[10]

Neither revolutionary nor republican but bourgeois liberal,
partisan of reforms in the framework of a constitutional
monarchy—such was the head of government under whose
authority Hegel was installed at Berlin. But this policy of
reform "à la Hardenberg" was in fact at the very forefront of the
struggle, and the reaction, in all its shades, was opposed to it.

Below we will discuss the *Burschenschaft*, whose political
orientation was shown to be very confused and equivocal.
Other than that, there was nothing that one could place as far to
the left as Chancellor Hardenberg. Along with his friends and
partisans, he constituted the principal bulwark against the
reactionary tendencies that found expression in the heart of his
own government. When he had disappeared along with his

colleagues, then the reaction seemed in fact to know restraint no longer.

In 1821 the German patriots placed almost all their hopes on him. They believed that he could achieve his whole program.

So it does not seem to us strictly necessary to reprimand Hegel for the letter of homage that he addressed to Hardenberg when forwarding his *Philosophy of Right*. He could be somewhat sincere in declaring that his intention in this work had been

> to grasp in its principal characteristics what lies before us to such great effect, the fruit of which we [now] enjoy.[11]

3. Altenstein

By and large the old Prince-Chancellor entrusted to his friend, the minister Altenstein, responsibility for the details of university affairs.

In 1818, with an appropriate mixture of respect and friendliness, Altenstein forwarded the definitive invitation to Hegel. He offered him Fichte's chair at the University of Berlin.

Recall that Altenstein had collaborated with Hardenberg during their shared exile in Riga. Hardenberg's treatise, which manifested such liberal tendencies, was itself inspired by a treatise of Altenstein. And when Hardenberg sent his document to the king he thought it well to enclose the one by Altenstein, possibly to assuage the fears of the sovereign about his plans by showing that much more frightening ones were possible.

For Altenstein went further than Hardenberg. He called for the suppression of the privileges of the nobility, which he felt ought to rest only on a distinction of birth and not on power or law. He advocated the abolition of serfdom; he was enthusiastic about economic liberalism and free enterprise. He condemned the guild system and proposed the suppression of ecclesiastical privileges, those "cushions for the lazy". He advised a complete reform of the army and declared in favour of representative assemblies of the people at each level of administration. He recommended municipal elections, the development of public education, the establishment of a university at Berlin.[12]

Altenstein's career certainly had its ups and downs. His period in the Ministry of Finance in 1808-10 was marked on the whole by failure, but could anyone else have mastered the terrible situation with which he was faced any better? Following a temporary retirement, he was called to Public Education in 1817. He entered into his true vocation.

An "enlightenment" man as well, as Niethammer stressed in a letter to Hegel,[13] he gave no evidence of a very profound faith, nor indeed of a very positive one. As one of his biographers said:

> he considered the quarrels of the Church from a point of view more philosophical and political than religious.[14]

Closest to his heart was popular education; the special importance that all bourgeois reformers gave to this question is well known. Altenstein's projects in this area ran up against powerful opposition. As much as possible he defended "academic freedom" against reactionary attacks; he protected teachers and students whom the police kept under surveillance and on occasion arrested.

However he did not proceed as he liked; far from it! Often he had to bend lest he be carried away by a contrary current. He delayed; he manoeuvred dangerously. Unable to implement his plans as a whole, he yet clung to power. He himself said to his colleagues: "If I go it will get worse."[15] In fact he was well aware what dangers threatened his work, and he preferred to remain in power at the price of some concessions to the aristocracy rather than to abandon the field entirely to them. They would have their revenge when he died and another minister, Eichhorn, took his place.

Following the defeat at Jena, the Prussian reformers rallied to the principle of compulsory schooling. Altenstein managed to implement it to some extent. In matters concerning the legislation and organization of schools Prussia led the way.

Altenstein seems to have been an intelligent, sensible and good man. He loved his country, and he detested the old social order. An example will show the type of person he ran afoul of.

One of the disgraceful features of his time was the employment of very young children in the factories. Managers delighted in using this cheap labour in mines and industries, and right from the start thereby destroyed countless lives. In industrial districts, the Prussian army could no longer recruit soldiers; young men able to bear arms were wanting; frightful conditions of labour during childhood had incapacitated them for the rest of their lives.

Compulsory education, Altenstein's ideal, came into direct conflict with the interests of the exploiters of child labour on this point. But he encountered political and ideological resistance as well, and Altenstein had to struggle against a coalition of sordid interests and regressive prejudices.

The aristocracy in fact dreaded the extension of public education, in which they discerned a powerful force for social emancipation. Even at the centre of government the school projects found little support except with Hardenberg. When Altenstein asked that managers be forbidden to employ children of less than eight years in their factories[16] he received from Schuckmann a rude response. The former Minister of Public Education, now Minister of the Interior, affirmed "that the work of children in factories is less injurious than work performed by the young for the purpose of acquiring culture."[17]

In his youth Altenstein had associated with free and bold spirits like Knebel, Hegel's friend at Jena, the publication of whose posthumous works by Varnhagen, the liberal man of letters and also a friend of Hegel, he later supported. A strange incident! The censor decided to ban the third volume of Knebel's *Works*, thus thwarting a project which the Minister of Public Education patronized.[18]

Under these conditions, how could we put Altenstein into the same category as the "restorers"? Here is how G. Weill characterized his work in the Ministry of Public Education. In Prussia, he said, the struggle over higher education

set two political parties in head-on collision: the modern bureaucrats who followed the tradition of Hardenberg, and the aristocracy who saw in religion a necessary support for the state against the revolutionary audacity of science and philosophy. The aristocracy hoped for several years to gain the upper hand with Frederick William III; but in 1817 he had chosen a new Minister of Public

Education, Altenstein, who would become the defender of the universities. Friend and protegé of Hardenberg, deeply interested in science, determined to make of Berlin the intellectual capital of Germany, Altenstein was viewed quite unfavourably by the reactionaries. Nevertheless an adept flexibility allowed him to traverse without damage the dark years following the Carlsbad decrees, and the valued assistance he gave for Frederick William III's great project – the reunion of the Protestant churches – assured him of the solid confidence of the old king. Altenstein continued to be minister for twenty-two years until his death. He it was who established the greatness of the University of Berlin. If he allowed fanatical orthodoxy to be installed at the faculty of theology with Hengstenberg, he protected the liberalism of Schleiermacher against all attacks. ... All in all, despite the continual denunciations of the orthodox and aristocrats who rejoiced in placing restrictions on Professor de Wette, despite the supervision of the curators appointed by the king, the Prussian universities retained under Altenstein the academic freedom of which they were proud.[19]

This judgement agrees more or less with that of Mehring, who wrote:

Altenstein was a friend of Hegel; not for nothing did he want to be Minister of Education in the state famous for compulsory education. His direction of school matters seemed to be the only relatively bright spot in the deficient administration of the Prussian state.[20]

Did not Engels himself acknowledge that Altenstein, "coming from a more liberal age, maintained a more advanced standpoint" than that of the other Prussian authorities?[21]

Those who failed to recognize Altenstein's liberalism during his life possibly missed it after his death. The new king, Frederick William IV, favoured pietism and political reaction more than his father. A. Cornu thus describes the ideological environment that was imposed:

The young Hegelians would become the first victims of this policy. Already Frederick William III, by the end of his reign, had turned more and more noticably against the Hegelians and against his minister Altenstein, who remained faithful to them and had great difficulty in defending them against attacks from orthodox and pietists. After the death of this minister, which happened in the spring of 1840 about the same time as that of Frederick William III, Hegelianism fell from favour, and the Hegelian left were persecuted.

Frederick William IV, who disliked the young Hegelians because of their liberal and anti-religious tendencies, named as successor to Altenstein the orthodox Eichhorn, who fought Hegelianism with as much zeal as his predecessor had defended it. The Hegelians were systematically dismissed from the university chairs; the reactionary jurist, Stahl, theoretician of absolutism, succeeded Gans, and the old Schelling was called to Berlin with the task of combatting and refuting Hegelianism.[22]

4. Schulze

But the patron closest at hand, at the same time Hegel's immediate superior and soon to be his disciple and friend, was the director of higher education in the Ministry of Education, Johannes Schulze (1786-1869).

No more a Prussian than his superiors, why did he place himself, as so many others had done, at Prussia's service? For reasons of the same kind. As a civil servant at Hanau at the beginning of the restoration, he witnessed the frantic efforts of the sovereign of the state of Hessen-Cassel to re-establish the pre-revolutionary order in its institutions and customs. He could not support this wave of reaction. To find a better political climate, he left for Berlin.

In his youth he had established all sorts of close relationships with compromising figures: Seume, the unfortunate author, well-known victim of German trafficking in soldiers; Rückert, the author of *Geharnischtes Sonette*; Görres,* at the very time that he was generating a stream of progressive ideas; Sinclair, Hegel's revolutionary friend;[23] Gneisenau,* the patriotic and bold general and theoretician of the people's war, whom the king, having used his services when in danger, quickly set aside[24]; and so on.

Schulze feared heresy hardly at all. He was a Freemason and was very active on its behalf. During his youth he had benefited from the patronage of the famous archbishop, Karl von Dalberg, whom Napoleon had named primate of the Rhineland Confederation. Liberal Protestant though he was, he had no qualms about dedicating a selection of his sermons in 1816 to this emancipated Catholic bishop. In 1808 he had been Talleyrand's guide during a visit to the Weimar library.

Hardenberg made his acquaintance on a trip through the Prussian Rhineland in 1817. He recommended him to Altenstein. In July 1818, Schulze became Director of Education.

No more than the others was he a revolutionary! But he was a fervent patriot, a friend of progress and a skilful organizer. Even though he served the Prussian monarchy, for want of a better, he did not approve of its obvious blemishes.

On one occasion he even reached the point of signing a "loyal address" to the throne, composed by Görres, which articulated the desire for a constitution. Persecuted because of his liberal ideas, Görres was soon seeking refuge in Strassburg. For his part, Schulze found himself faced with censure.

Even after obtaining the post of Director in the Ministry of Education he was not successful in avoiding all suspicion. So in 1819, in the course of a circuit of inspection, he met by chance (at least so he claimed) the Grand-duke of Saxe-Weimar, Karl August, whose territories served as a refuge and defence for democrats and advanced thinkers. The conversation bore precisely—also as if by chance!—on the measures that the Prussian government was beginning to bring against those who opposed it, those it called "the demagogues." The campaign of repression begun in Prussia had already provoked some friction with Saxe-Weimar.

Schulze declared himself hostile to these "anti-demagogue" persecutions; he found them exaggerated and unjustified. But spies from the Prussian police managed to hear this conversation with Karl August. They prepared a report that went right to the king. Schulze had to submit to interrogation. He succeeded in proving the purely accidental character, neither pre-meditated nor conspiratorial, of his encounter with the Duke of Weimar. However he was watched from then on, and through the years he felt that he was suspected of complicity with the "demagogues".[25]

At Berlin Schulze attended a whole series of Hegel's courses; he protected the Hegelians, and after the death of the master, he participated with Gans, Förster and others in the first edition of his complete works. He enjoyed Hegel's company. When passing through Dresden in 1824, he postponed his departure so that he could have some extra time with the philosopher who had just arrived in town. Together they went to see their friend Böttiger—and this at the very moment when, in this same town of Dresden, the sensational arrest of Victor Cousin was being planned.[26]

Neither Hegel nor his disciples needed to blush on account of the assistance Schulze extended to them. It came from a man passionately devoted to the cause of public education and the democratic extension of culture; it came from a man who welcomed political reforms. Because he did not belong to the nobility, Schulze no doubt represented better than Hardenberg and Altenstein the type of competent and disinterested civil servant in whom Hegel saw the principal support of the state.

Let us mention still another person who played an important role in the nomination of Hegel by sending a quite favourable report to Schuckmann in 1816. This was the historian, von Raumer (1781-1873).

In an anonymous publication of 1805, he wrote an apology for economic liberalism. He became associated with Hardenberg in 1810, and because he exercised a measure of influence over him he was called "the little chancellor". Here is what Cavaignac says:

> Frederick von Raumer became the deputy of the chancellor. He was then 29 years of age; he was born near Dessau and had made a speedy advance in the Prussian administration. He was one of those deputies that Hardenberg loved to have around him. With an open mind and facile pen, very able in serving as the instrument of Hardenberg's lively and active mind, he had nevertheless his own personal ideas and tendencies. Much more a writer than an administrator, very curious about matters of the mind, very open to the movement of ideas, imbued with the need for a complete renovation and for the supression of the abuses of the old order, he would have been like most of the Prussian administrators of his time, personally taken with imitating English models.[27]

Around 1811, withdrawing for a time from active political life, Raumer devoted himself to important historical work on the middle ages. Nevertheless, he did not lose contact with current affairs. In 1832 he published a book on *The Fall of Poland* (*Polands Untergang*) which evoked displeasure in the court and with the king.

Later he intervened in the religious struggles, and gave evidence of his liberalism on this occasion as well. In 1847 he gave a discourse on tolerance which so strongly displeased the king and the court that he had to surrender his position as Secretary of the Academy.

Considered a kind of martyr for his convictions, he was elected as a deputy after the revolution of 1848. One can see that Raumer no more fits into the definition of a reactionary, nor even into that of a conservative, than do Hardenberg, Altenstein or Schulze,

5. The Prussian Bureaucracy

All of these Prussian "semi-reformers" who supported Hegel, and whom Hegel supported, were quite different from the French revolutionaries of 1793. But is it even appropriate to compare them in this way? They did not go beyond middle class demands as did the Montagnards.[28] Indeed they did not go quite that far.

They lived in a different situation and in their own way struggled under very different social and political conditions. We need to judge them in comparison with their contemporaries. In this context the progressive thrust they shared was of the utmost significance.

Most of the Germans who had begun by admiring the French Revolution ended by entering the ranks of extreme reaction. Think, for example, of Stolberg, Schelling, Görres himself, as well as many others!

Only a few individuals, isolated moreover from the bulk of their nation and somewhat disconcerted by the unforeseen course of events, remained faithful to the methods and manner of the French Revolution, to its general orientation at least, to its inspiration, and to the new spirit that had given it life. They espoused an ideal of rationality, of culture and of progress.

Some of these, indeed not a few, belonged to what is generally called the Prussian "bureaucracy": in particular Hegel's patrons, civil servants in the Prussian administration.

Hegel has been accused of placing too much confidence in them. "Hegel," says H. Sée, "saw hope for the future only in a Prussian-type bureaucracy."[29]

In fact, as we shall soon demonstrate, Hegel frequently disobeyed the orders of the governing bureaucracy, even though he felt great admiration for the body of civil servants as a whole.

The word "bureaucracy" has a disagreeable sound to French ears. By wedding "bureaucracy" with "Prussia" one creates delightfully terrifying effects. However, it is worth taking objective account of the qualities of this bureaucracy: conscientious, meticulous, concerned for public welfare; that is the way it appeared to Hegel.

At the time it was practically the only political force that resisted the feudal hierarchy. Its members worked to give new life to the country, and as a result they came into conflict with special interests, with outdated regulations, with mediaeval customs. In addition they recruited from the middle class, or from the "enlightened" nobility, spiritual cousins of the bourgeoisie.

The rare Prussian revolutionary of the 18th and beginning of the 19th century came from their ranks: for example, the directors of the conspiracy of the *Evergetes*, certainly well known to Hegel.[30]

A certain "radicalism" frequently showed itself in the Prussian bureaucracy during the decades following the French Revolution.[31] A number of contemporaries understood it to be quite other than a simple tool of monarchic absolutism. Thus J.A. Eberhard, whose books Hegel read,[32] believed in 1798 that there was no need of a revolution in Prussia because in this country, in contrast to France, authority

> found a sufficient counterweight in its admirable bureaucracy which knew how, if need be, to oppose the orders of the king and to enlighten him concerning the real interests of the nation.[33]

An opinion such as this rested on serious illusions about the real nature of the Prussian state. These, however, were grafted on to reality, certain characteristics of which they exaggerated rather than invented completely. There was indeed in the Prussia of this time a state and an administration relatively more independent of the upper classes, perhaps, than at any other time or place. In this respect Marx and Engels point out in *The German Ideology* that

> the impotence of each separate sphere of life (one can speak here neither of estates nor of classes, but at most of former estates, and of classes not yet born) did not allow any one of them to gain exclusive domination. The inevitable consequence was that during the epoch of absolute monarchy, which assumed here its most stunted, semi-patriarchal form, the special sphere which, owing to division of labour, was responsible for the administration of public interests acquired an abnormal independence, which became still greater in the bureaucracy of modern times. Thus the state built itself up into an apparently independent force, and this position, which in other countries was only transitory—a passing stage—it has maintained in Germany until the present day.[34]

Let us not make the mistake of oversimplifying the relations between Hegel and the Prussian state. Relatively free of the ascendancy of a single social class, this state could yet not pride itself on having complete homogeneity. Diverse and antagonistic social groups struggled for dominance; among the most important were the feudal lords, the middle class, the lower middle class, and the bureaucracy, formed as it was into a relatively autonomous body.

This basic conflict emerged in a great number of fragmentary and secondary quarrels; in these the different parties intervened in various ways, depending on which questions were in dispute.

The political tendencies here did not offer the same neatness and definiteness of contour as did those which were placed face to face in the French Revolution. But in the last analysis, when it came to essentials each class recognized and followed its own orientation just the same.

Now Hegel went to the side of Altenstein, Schulze, Varnhagen and Förster; he did not let himself be drawn into the side of Schuckmann, Wittgenstein, Eichhorn and company.

6. The "Philosopher of the State"

Thanks to the protection in high places just mentioned, one-sided though it be, did Hegel succeed in subordinating philosophical instruction, indeed all instruction, to his own authority? He has frequently been accorded the honour (or the shame) of having done so. Doubtless inspired by Lucien Herr and others we have cited, René Maublanc thought he could affirm that Hegel "from 1818 to his death ... exercised a sort of dictatorship over thought and teaching in Prussia."[35]

Quite obviously Hegel did not arrive in Berlin crowned with a sufficient aura of prestige to assume such omnipotence from the beginning. But perhaps, thanks to favoritism, he acquired it subsequently? An easily understandable favoritism, according to Flint, who writes:

> It is not astonishing that the Prussian government of the time with its cavalier treatment of radicals and reformers had greatly admired this way of viewing reality through rose-coloured glasses; and that it had filled the Churches and philosophy chairs in the universities with men prepared to teach such an agreeable and obliging doctrine.[36]

How many errors in so few words! What lack of understanding!

Could Flint really confuse "viewing reality through rose-coloured glasses" in his words with "recognizing reason as the rose in the cross of the present", as Hegel recommended doing?*

As for the "cavalier treatment of radicals and reformers", we will later discover how things really were. For the moment, however, let us ask if the "Prussian government" actually imposed Hegel's philosophy on the intellectual world, using authoritarian means to do so.

We know already, in any case, that in the last analysis it could involve only the support given to Hegel by *one* government minister, Altenstein — and also by Hardenberg, before his sudden death in 1822.

Now the support of Altenstein and of his subordinates like Schulze appears neither excessive nor unjust. In fact, it mainly consisted in protection in the face of arbitrary and reactionary attacks, a protection often ineffectual, proportionate to the real power Altenstein exercised in the corridors of government.

Hegel saw himself endowed with no omnipotence in the realm of philosophy and education. Only rarely and with difficulty did his patrons succeed in sparing his disciples the harrassment of censorship and the police.

Certainly, several of Hegel's students were successful in finding places and securing tenure in the Prussian university. But on the other hand, how many unfortunate, persecuted Hegelians there were.

Better than a long and detailed analysis, some examples will help us assess the extent of Hegel's "dictatorial" powers.

In 1818 the philosopher wanted to have as an assistant for his own courses the person of Carové, a disciple from Heidelberg. The project ran afoul of petty regulations. Hegel did not succeed in acquiring for his own student an official nomination; the great philosopher turned out to be unable to appoint the assistant of his choice!

Carové, a devoted Hegelian, then undertook to tutor privately and without official remuneration in his master's courses. The attempt was rudely interrupted in 1819. Following the publication of Carové's pamphlet on the Sand affair, the police initiated an investigation and arrested Hegel's assistant. From then on the fury of the feudal nobility pursued him without respite. Police, the courts and the "Commission of Mainz" were at the heels of this "demagogue".

Excluded from the University of Berlin, prevented from having access to any university function, watched by the police, he would at first obtain but a very mediocre job in the service of the Cologne customs. Subsequently, quite destitute, he would devote himself to private publishing.

Thus did the Prussian reaction break the career, and indeed the life, of a young, promising intellectual, the first one chosen by Hegel to interpret his thought at Berlin, a man whom he tried to defend as much as possible in the face of persecution, for whom he always maintained his esteem, and with whom he never broke off friendly, though compromising, relations.[37]

With Carové out of the picture, Hegel took an assistant whose personal situation corresponded to the requirements of the regulation, and who was officially appointed: von Henning.

What happened to this second disciple? A letter from Hegel to Niethammer laconically gives us the news:

> For one year now a teaching assistant has been made available to me
> for my lectures. His job is to attend my lectures and then go over
> them with the students four hours a week. ... He was under arrest for
> ten weeks on suspicion of demagoguery, with a gendarme guarding
> him day and night in prison.[38]

At the very moment the *Philosophy of Right* appeared — the
work that is now accused of servilely backing the authorities —
the police were hardly sparing of Hegel's assistants.

Von Henning, a close friend of Carové and of all sorts of
other suspects, equally intimate with Hegel, could subsequently
never obtain a certificate of innocence from the Prussian
courts.[39]

He would participate in the first edition of the complete
works of Hegel. Later, long after the death of the master, he
would rejoin the camp of orthodoxy and absolutism.

One convinced Hegelian had the good fortune of teaching
at Berlin at the same time as his master, and under his
direction. He took a leading role in founding the *Jahrbücher für
wissenschaftliche Kritik*, the organ of the Hegelian school. He
too contributed a great deal to the edition of the complete
works: that was the jurist Eduard Gans (1797-1839).

Son of a Jewish merchant with whom Hardenberg had
developed a friendship, he had, like so many of his
co-religionists, paid the entry fees for civil and university life by
converting officially to Christianity.[40] He became "professor
extraordinary" in 1815, then full professor in 1828.

In 1825 Hegel entrusted him with teaching the philosophy
of law. A congenial and, from many points of view, fascinating
personality, Gans encountered an enthusiastic response from
the students, and contributed quite actively to spreading
Hegel's ideas. A crowd of auditors thronged his lectures; never
had such popularity been known in the halls of the University of
Berlin.[41]

Gans was a propagandist for liberal ideas. He is
occasionally presented as a sort of apostle, thinking of nothing
but freedom, progress and the new spirit. Admirer of the
French Revolution, friend of Heine, frequenting the liberal
salon of Varnhagen,[42] he always remained Hegel's faithful
disciple.

Hegel was soon to know the same unpleasantness with Gans as with Carové and Henning. The crown prince himself one day gave him a warning about the liberal jurist: "It is a scandal, Professor, that Professor Gans makes all our students into republicans!"

Hegel excused himself by claiming ... that he did not know the content of Gans's lectures! But knowing well enough from experience what dangers were involved in an observation of this sort, he promised to resume teaching the philosophy of law himself from the following semester.[43]

If he had lived a little longer he would have seen his favorite disciple suffer the same persecution as Carové. Gans's lectures were banned and he was dismissed. In 1839 his funeral became the occasion for a kind of demonstration of political opposition.

These three examples, which cover the whole period of Hegel's teaching at Berlin, suffice to restore the proper value – minimal – to the "favoritism" from which he is supposed to have profited together with his disciples; to the "dictatorship" which he is supposed to have imposed on the university, and to the "servility" of his "officially imposed" doctrine, as Lucien Herr has it.

In fact Altenstein had difficulty in maintaining "academic freedom". It took some effort to prevent Hegel's friends from being systematically removed from the university. He had only limited power at his disposal. Hegel, the great Hegel, could not gain admittance to the Berlin Academy of Science, and the scientific journal he founded did not obtain the official patronage that, against Gans's advice, he craved for it.

We shall not espouse the opinion of Harich according to whom "Hegel's philosophy was the dominant intellectual force in Prussia at the time of the restoration."[44]

What is meant by "the dominant intellectual force"? If it be a matter of an appreciation of the value of Hegel's philosophy, it is self-evident; there was nothing comparable to set at its side.

On the other hand, if one is thinking of an expanding influence, as doubtless Harich is, if one is assessing an ideological force and its influence on public opinion, then Hegel's thought could not claim to have won out over the others – at least from the standpoint of the philosopher himself.

How can we forget the sway of Protestant orthodoxy, and its almost exclusive domination of the great mass of the Prussian people? The reactionaries brought it to the fore at court, and in the homes of the nobles, the peasants and the lower middle class. The most diverse and most widespread social spheres knew nothing at all about Hegel, his name or his doctrine, which marked out a path only in the narrow circle of intellectuals and business men.

To be sure, Marx in 1843 declared that the writings of Hegel were officially propagated, and that the public reproached him with being Prussia's "state philosopher". But what public? Marx adds that Hegel taught the philosophy of law in 1831 "by a special order of government".[45] But we have just seen in what circumstances.

The text of Marx in which these statements occur is violently polemical. It contests the legitimacy of the censorship of the *Rheinische Zeitung* by opposing a diversity of possible opinions on the constitution to a dogmatic judgement. On this question, as Marx himself points out, "Stein, Hardenberg and Schön had one opinion and Rochow, Arnim and Eichhorn another."[46]

Marx could not have doubted that the party in government which supported Hegel was connected with Stein, Hardenberg, and Schön! And in 1821 it was "in the minority."

In an essay where he assumed a more historical point of view, Engels defined the extent and the variations in the real influence of Hegel's philosophy:

> The works he had published were all couched in a rigorously scientific, almost thorny style, and, like the *Jahrbücher für wissenschaftliche Kritik* where his students wrote in the same manner, could count on only a small audience of scholars who were, moreover, already predisposed to them. ... The influence of Hegel's lectures always remained limited to a small circle. ... But with Hegel's death his philosophy really began to come alive. The publication of his collected works, particularly the lectures, had a profound effect.[47]

Hegel attracted to his following the best minds, but not the greatest number. His adversaries, Ancillon, Haller, Savigny and Stahl also founded schools. The partial success that the Hegelian doctrine knew at the beginning of the 19th century was acquired by its own merit. Why should one be astonished at the seduction it exercised over several intellects among the elite?

One has to be glad that Altenstein, in naming Hegel to Berlin, had *recognized* his merit. Posterity confirms his judgement. Compared to Hegel, his rivals were pygmies. It could have been Fries, rather than Hegel, who occupied the chair of philosophy at Berlin.

After Hegel's death they searched out the old Schelling to combat Hegelianism, and to try to recall those whom Hegel had evidently urged ahead. The authority of the court, of the nobility, of the least progressive parties in government exerted themselves *against* Hegel. Replying to the accusations that Haym[48] had made, Schulze protested:

> It would not be difficult for me, by citing facts, to convince you that Hegel never did enjoy special favoritism from government here, that he never came close to being a slave of the reaction that had its start at the Congress of Aix-la-Chapelle, and that the reproach of having made his system the intellectual and spiritual home of the so-called Prussian reaction does not apply.[49]

NOTES

1. *Briefe*, II, 31-32; *Letters*, 294. An indication of the political attitudes of Sinclair will be found in our study, *Hegel secret*, Part 3, Chapter II.

2. On this point see Aug. Fournier, *Historische Studien und Skizzen*, (Prague & Leipzig, 1885) Bd. I, *Illuminaten und Patrioten*, 292n.

3. *Briefe*, II, 193; *Letters*, 633.

4. On the liberal and progressive features of the Hegelian conception of the state, see E. Weil, *Hegel et l'état*, (Paris, 1951).

5. See my *Hegel secret*, Part I, Chapter 2.

6. Texts of Hardenberg from G. Winter, *Die Reorganization des Preussischen Staats unter Stein und Hardenberg*, Bd. I, (Leipzig, 1931) 305ff.

7. See Cavaignac, *La Formation de la Prusse contemporaire*, (Paris, 1898) II, 64; as well as G. Weill, *L'Eveil des Nationalités*, (Paris, 1930) 47: "A muffled and opinionated struggle took place in the court of Frederick William

between the Chancellor, always influential, and the absolutist party, which distrusted this 'Jacobin'."

8. Cavaignac. *op.cit.* I, 341.

9. Ibid. 342-343.

10. F. Mehring, *Historische Aufsätze...*, 220-221.

11. *Briefe*, II 242; *Letters*, 459. Hegel must have been aware in addition of another aspect of the Chancellor's personality: Hardenberg worked for the political emancipation of the Jews, not without success, and he strove to spare them from persecution. On this point see L. Geiger, *Geschichte der Juden in Berlin*, (Berlin, 1871) 142 and 150.

12. See *Allgemeine Deutsche Biographie*, "Altenstein," 646.

13. *Briefe* II, 209.

14. *Allgemeine Deutsche Bibliographie*, "Altenstein," 652.

15. Ibid. 656. On the movement of reaction in the university after Altenstein's death, see Cornu, *K. Marx et F. Engels* (Paris, 1955) I, 168.

16. See G. Weill, *L'Eveil des nationalités* (Paris, 1930) 359.

17. See F. Mehring, *op. cit.* 248.

18. See P. Reimann, *Hauptströmung der deutschen Literatur 1750-1848*, (Berlin, 1956) 185f.

19. G. Weill, *op.cit.* 212.

20. F. Mehring, *op.cit.* 248.

21. F. Engels, *Ernst Moritz Arndt*, in Marx-Engels: *Collected Works* (New York, 1975) II, 143.

22. A. Cornu, *K. Marx et F. Engels* (Paris, 1955) I, 169.

23. See Käthe Hengsberger, *Isaak von Sinclair, ein Freund Hölderlins* (Germanisches Studien No. 5) (Berlin, 1920) 79-82.

24. On Gneisenau, "the man of genius," see Engels, *Preussische Franktireurs* (December, 1870) in *MEW*, Bd. 17, (Berlin, 1962) 205ff.

25. See Kuno Fischer, *op.cit.* 136-137.

26. See *Briefe* III, 48; *Letters*, 610. Böttiger had been one of the most active and most obstinate Illuminati of Bavaria. (On this point see *Hegel Secret*.)

27. Cavaignac, *op.cit.* II, 49.

28. See Engels, *Socialism: Utopian and Scientific*, Introduction to the English edition: "In order to secure even those conquests of the bourgeoisie that were ripe for gathering at the time, the revolution had to be carried considerably further—exactly as in 1793 in France and 1848 in Germany. This seems, in fact, to be one of the laws of evolution of bourgeois society." [tr. E. Aveling (New York, 1972) 18.]

29. H. Sée, "Remarques sur la philosophie de l'histoire de Hegel," *Revue d'histoire de la philosophie*, 1927, 327n3.

30. Frommann, Hegel's publisher friend, was a participant. On the conspiracy see Droz, *L'Allemagne et la Revolution Française* (Paris, 1949) 96-97. See also my *Hegel secret*.

31. See Droz, *op. cit.* 103.

32. See *Dokumente zu Hegels Entwicklung*, ed. Hoffmeister (Stuttgart, 1936) 144.

33. Droz, *op. cit.* 109.

34. Marx and Engels, *The German Ideology*, in *Collected Works* (New York, 1975) I, 195. See also page 90.

35. R. Maublanc, *La Philosophie du marxisme et l'enseignement officiel* (Paris, 1935) 14n1.

36. Flint, *La Philosophie de l'histoire en Allemagne*, tr. Carrau, (Paris, 1878) 316.

37. See *Briefe* II, 455-468, notes of Hoffmeister. The last known letter from Carové to Hegel dates from November, 1830. (*Briefe* III, 316.)

38. *Briefe* II, 271; *Letters*, 470.

39. See Hegel, *Berliner Schriften* (Hamburg, 1956) 598, note by Hoffmeister.

40. On the attitude of orthodox Jews towards a "conversion" agreed to in such circumstances, see L. Geiger, *Geschichte der Juden in Berlin* (Berlin, 1871) 179f.

41. See L. Geiger, *op. cit.*, p. 587. During the winter semester of 1829-30, 201 students attended Gans's classes, and 166 attended those of Hegel. To his public lectures, soon to be banned, Gans gathered more than 1500. See Saint-Marc Girardin, in his preface to Gans's *Histoire du droit de succession en France au moyen âge*, Paris, 1845, p. xi.

42. See Spenlé, *Rahel Varnhagen* (Paris, 1910) 195, 199, 213, etc.

43. *Briefe* III 472, Hoffmeister's note 1.

44. Introduction to an edition of Heine's text: *Zur Geschichte der Deutschen Philosophie* (Berlin, 1956) 5.

45. K. Marx, "Marginal Notes to the Accusations of the Ministerial Rescript," Marx-Engels, *Collected Works* I, 362.

46. Ibid.

47. Engels, "Schelling and Revelation," in Marx-Engels, *Collected Works* II, 195.

48. R. Haym, *Hegel und seine Zeit* (Berlin, 1857).

49. Cited in G.E. Müller, *Hegel*, (Bern/Munich, 1959) 304. The evidence of a further contemporary witness on this point, that of Varnhagen, is cited in the same work, p. 305.

V

Enemies

1. The King, the Court and the Crown Prince

There was a powerful force confronting the reforming ministers, the patriotic civil servants and the liberal academics: the court! And a king who, after long following the advice of Hardenberg, let himself be more and more indoctrinated by Metternich, and who inclined more and more towards the side of the court and of the reactionary tutors who educated the crown prince.

It seems that Hegel attracted the hatred of the court right from the start of his sojourn in Berlin. Yet Prince William invited him to dinner once, in 1818.* On account of his reputation? or of his position? It could be that the philosopher owed the favour as much to the interest of Princess Wilhelmina, born Marianne of Hesse-Homburg.

She was the daughter of Frederick V, protector and friend of Isaac von Sinclair; during the dinner the princess and the philosopher recalled memories of this strange companion of their youth.[1]

As far as we know, such a princely invitation was renewed only rarely. We can establish the date of just one other meeting, in 1831, which the crown prince used to attack Gans's teaching.[2] By virtue of everything in his education and of his well-known political opinions, the prince was quite unfavourably disposed to Hegel's philosophy.

The king himself remained attached to absolutism. It was only due to fear that he allowed some concessions to the politics of Stein and Hardenberg. If he did express some sympathy for Hegelian ideas, it can be explained only by his proverbial lack of intelligence.

Yet, not having penetrated the spirit of the system, in which he was scarcely interested, he nevertheless recognized its consequences, which too clearly posed dangers for him. A courtier once told him that Hegel in his theory granted to the king simply the right to "dot the i".[3] The sovereign replied: "And what if the king does not dot it?" He had at least understood within what narrow limits Hegel wanted to restrict his freedom to manoeuvre![4]

Another incident helps us grasp the nature of the relations between the philosopher and the court.

In the time after he settled in Berlin, Hegel's philosophy brought its author a certain acclaim from a narrow range of specialists. But in addition the congenial personality of the philosopher could establish a rapport which his abstruse thought could not achieve.

His administrative activities put him in contact with people of all sorts. He went out a lot, was a regular at literary salons, loved good conversation and the theatre, played cards, and associated easily with his fellows. He soon could count on several disciples, as well as a much larger number of cordial, though not close, friends.

In 1826 several of these, in association with some students, decided to celebrate his birthday in a special way. Recalling that Goethe's birthday fell on the very next day after Hegel's, they decided to combine the two dates by means of a night of merry-making. They organized a small banquet. The professor received poems, gifts, and testimonials of admiration.

This display of affection breathed sincerity. It profoundly touched Hegel. He shared the experience immediately with his wife, at that time absent from Berlin:

You will not believe what warm, deeply-felt testimonies of confidence, affection, and respect have been shown to my by these dear friends -- the mature ones and the younger men alike. It has been a rewarding day for the many troubles of life.[5]

If people describe Hegel's life at Berlin as constant success, it is in no small part due to this little celebration:

Each year (Roques tells us) his birthday was a triumph: gifts, speeches, appropriate poems, nothing was lacking. In 1830 a medal was struck.[6]

Nevertheless something is missing, if not from the celebration, at least from the picture given of it. It lacks the king's anger.

A detail of Roques' text is unintentionally ironic: "each year"!...

In fact, never again was Hegel's birthday celebrated so publicly and so warmly. The next year, 1827, on the date of his birthday, Hegel judged it more prudent to be absent from Berlin....

The celebration of 1826 did not pass unnoticed. The *Vossische Zeitung* published a sympathetic account of the merry-making. Then it suddenly transpired that they had forgotten one thing: if Hegel's birthday was just before Goethe's, it was also not too far from the birthday of Frederick William, and seemed to be competing with it.

Ridiculous and unbelievable as it would seem today, the king was jealous. The birthdays of the "great pagan" of Weimar and of the Berlin philosopher had resulted in too magnificent a display of sympathy and admiration.

Hegel's enemies at court cried scandal. And this is what Varnhagen notes on the subject:

What irritated them particularly was the description of the celebration as it was given in the *Vossische Zeitung*. In a cabinet decree the king has now ordered the office of censorship to ensure that similar articles on private celebrations do not find a place in the papers. It appears that it is taken to be improper to treat with such importance any celebration other than those for the royal family or for dignitaries. ... 'Philosophy, though still well considered by the

state, should beware! The court may still threaten it; and Hegel is no
safer than anyone else!'[7]

Hegel understood the warning. The following year he sadly
celebrated his birthday all alone in a distant inn, a stage on his
journey to Paris.[8]   But by thus escaping from such paltry
vexations he only exposed himself to other troubles.   He was
suspected of having undertaken the trip to bring to a successful
conclusion some projects of political opposition.[9]

So much for Hegel's annual triumph!

Now, to appreciate better the relative daring of his political
ideas between 1820 and 1831, let us compare them with those
the crown prince espoused and, twenty years later, solemnly
proclaimed, after having become Frederick William IV, King of
Prussia.

He had been educated politically by the reactionary
Ancillon, in the presence of Count von Stolberg, more
reactionary still. But he knew how to surpass his teacher and, in
all essentials, adopted the theory of Haller, the philosopher of
the restoration, with whom Hegel took such lively issue in the
Philosophy of Right.[10]

In 1842, responding to a timidly liberal pamphlet by von
Schön, Frederick William IV set forth the principles of royal
sovereignty as he conceived them. They explicitly contradict
Hegel's public theory.

Frederick William affirmed: "I feel myself king solely by the
grace of God and with his aid will remain so to the end."

One recalls that, in his oral commentary on the *Philosophy
of Right*, edited by Gans, Hegel made the ironical remark:

> If we are to grasp the idea of the monarch, we cannot be satisfied
> with saying that God has appointed kings to rule over us, since God
> has done everything, even the worst of things.[11]

In the Hegelian theory, the justification of the monarchy
owed nothing to divine grace.   Frederick William added
menacingly:

> Be assured on my royal word. In my time no lord, no servant, no
> provincial assembly and no band of Jewish intellectuals will

appropriate anything which at present belongs either justly or unjustly to the Crown, unless I have previously made an offer of it..."

Such words stand far removed from those of Hegel concerning the rationality of the State, concerning the abolition of "good pleasure" and of individual arbitrariness, and concerning the legitimacy of property.

Prince von Hardenberg found himself retroactively classed among the usurping servants. Projects for national represention and expectations of a constitution were disavowed. The king even placed under accusation the "band of Jewish intellectuals" which, in the persons of Rahel Varnhagen, the banker Block, Heinrich Beer, the Mendelssohns, Gans, and various Jewish actors and composers, had constituted one of Hegel's favored associations.

The King of Prussia continued:

A patriarchal government is the German type of leadership [for Hegel patriarchies were a style of life and a system of institutions quite out of date], and since sovereign authority is my paternal heritage, my patrimony, therefore I have my people at heart, therefore I can and will direct those of my subjects who, like children in their minority, need it, punish the degenerate, but in contrast offer a share in the administration of my goods to the worthy and the well brought up, assign to them their own patrimony, and defend them from the presumption of servants.[12]

Clearly, the monarch wanted to strike the French Revolution from the records!

Those who were contemporary to that great event did not regard the problems it posed and solved as we now do. For them the question of the political minority of the people continued to be of major importance.

Many apprehensive doctrinaire thinkers maintained the eternal minority of the people. Thus, in 1816, Ancillon held that

the people have the need to be governed like children; for both have the need to be protected, educated and improved.[13]

On the other hand progressive minds, Hegel among them, rejected the idea of this minority (*Unmündigkeit*) of man. Even in the writings of his youth he declared that

> human nature, with the degree of perfection demanded of it, is too dignified to be placed at the level of nonage where it would always need a guardian and could never enter the status of manhood.[14]

Again, in the *Lectures on the Philosophy of History* he affirmed that

> In these cases people demand, if they are to exert themselves in any direction, that the object should commend itself to them; that in point of opinion—whether as to its goodness, justice, advantage, profit—they should be able to 'enter into it' (*dabei seyn*). This is a consideration of especial importance in our age, when people are less than formerly influenced by reliance on others, and by authority; when, on the contrary, they devote their activities to a cause on the ground of their own understanding, their independent conviction and opinion.[15]

To treat "subjects ... like children" is the mark of despotism.[16]

In the kind of political manifesto which we have cited from Frederick William IV there is nothing that moves in the direction that Hegel took. His constant vindication of Frederick II, the philosopher king, would not please the new sovereign either.

In Frederick II, Hegel celebrated the "hero of Protestantism", who did not get lost in theological quarrels, but who "took up the Protestant principle in its secular aspect."[17] In the same vein, in Hegel's lectures on the French Encyclopaedists in his *History of Philosophy*, he defended Frederick II from the posthumous attacks to which he had been subjected.[18] And that at a time when any praise of Frederick II was increasingly considered to be a type of revolutionary manifesto![19]

Hegel did not view the state as the property of the king, nor law as the result of the sovereign's arbitrary decision. One should read again the marginal notes to Paragraph 75 in the *Philosophy of Right*:

The state... – no longer the ruler's private property, the ruler's private right – ... domains have become the property of the state. Justice – no longer patrimonial jurisdiction...." and so on.[20]

Republicans might well have been irritated with all that the *Philosophy of Right* retained that was monarchical. Von Thaden wrote to Hegel: "You are decried by turns as a 'royalist philosopher', and a 'philosophical royalist'."[21]

But as Engels wrote in 1850 in a text that Marx allowed to be published under his own name, and which was attributed to him for a long time:

> There was then no separate republican party in Germany. People were either Constitutional monarchists, or more or less clearly defined Socialists or Communists.[22]

To say nothing, naturally, of the absolutists! ... But Engels was thinking of the period just after that of Hegel. ...

In 1820 neither socialists nor communists had made their appearance in Germany. The boldest reformers of the time called for the introduction of a constitutional monarchy. Hegel developed a "rational theory" about it, one in which true monarchists saw real monarchy being dissipated. And they were enraged by this insolent treatment!

2. Theorists of the Restoration

Who, then, were the thinkers in Berlin who argued for reaction when Hegel refused to do so? There were many. A whole set of theorists opposed the revolutionary movement, endlessly extended and elaborated their indictment of the French Revolution, and propounded opinionated arguments against all projects of reform.

Among their leaders we should first mention Friedrich Ancillon (1767-1837), member of the Academy of Science, tutor of the crown prince, and one of the prime movers of the reactionary party at court. He participated actively in the struggle against Hardenberg's proposals for a constitution, and urged the king to follow ever more closely the politics of Metternich.[23]

In 1816 he published his study of *Sovereignty and Political Constitutions.*[24]   Ancillon did not break entirely with rationalism, and several traces of ideas from the 18th century may yet be found in his work. Thus he recognized in man "an unlimited capacity for perfection",[25] and he referred frequently to Montesquieu.[26]

But he compared the people to children in their minority;[27] he denied that sovereignty came from the people; he praised the nobility who guaranteed, together with the hereditary monarchy, the permanence of the state; he justified the Junkers' possession of large entailed estates.[28]

He submitted the notion of the *spirit of the times* (*Zeitgeist*), so Hegelian and so dear to Hardenberg, to violent attack: "The spirit of the times," he asserted, "can be neither purely rational, nor strictly moral."[29] He condemned the French Revolution in its entirety, Napoleon included, as a political monstrosity which God's justice had fortunately terminated.[30] On the other side, he sang the praises of the middle ages and their secular institutions.[31] He concluded his treatise with a vindication of the Holy Alliance and of the spirit of contemporary monarchs, "more critical for the future of Europe than any written constitution whatever!"[32]

Yet Ancillon appeared a moderate beside K.L. von Haller (1768-1854), who surpassed him in force of convictions, in vigor of expression, and in anti-revolutionary rancour. From 1816 on there appeared the successive volumes of Haller's work: *The Restoration of the Political Sciences.*[33] This restoration of the political sciences openly declared itself to be a political science of the restoration.

We cannot provide a detailed exposition of Haller's theory; several quotations will at least suffice to reveal its flavour. The author proclaimed his hatred for any constitution:

This word [he wrote] is poison in monarchies, a corpse-like word, which brings corruption with it and spreads the smell of death.[34]

Haller issued a call to war against "the godless sect of the liberals", he was fanatically obsessed with the memory of the French Revolution, with the Enlightenment, with Free Masonry. He preached "unconditional obedience" to subjects, and allowed limitless power to sovereigns. Rare though it was at the time, he even took up the defence of the Inquisition.[35]

Haller spelled out the state of his dreams: the *Patrimonial State*. According to him, genuine relations between sovereign and subject ought to be based on a patriarchal model. The throne, the country, and the inhabitants form the private property of the sovereign, inalienable and hereditary.

Haller provided the Junkers with a justification for their embittered resistance to agrarian reform; he condemned every limitation of seigneurial rights. For him the domination of the strong over the weak, of the king over the nation and of the lord over his people had the force of an eternal law, upon which the state itself is established.[36]

The profoundly reactionary character of Haller's theories is well enough known. What is less known, generally, is the role this theoretician played in Prussian political life around 1820. The court at Berlin, naturally enough, approved of Haller and granted him its support. The crown prince delighted in his works, and borrowed from them principles for his own political stance.

But the philosophy of Haller, who was a Swiss aristocrat, evoked but little sympathy even in his own city of Berne, where he was, however, a member of the Grand Council. In the Swiss capital they were less reactionary in 1820 than they had been at the very end of the 18th century. They even tried to exclude Haller from the Grand Council, but they gave up the first attempt under pressure from the Prussian ambassador, Haller's protector on this occasion.[37] This information is important for us. It leaves no doubt that, in attacking Haller, Hegel took on — with fierce intensity — the noble councillors, intimates of the king, the teachers of the crown prince, and in particular the crown prince himself.

At the same time Hegel's attack touched Metternich, who did not hesitate to take a personal interest in Haller's cause whenever it was actually threatened.

In 1820 Haller published a work: *On the Constitution of the Spanish Cortes*, in which he condemned with his usual vehemence the new Spanish institutions. The major German courts, who were quite disturbed about the change happening in Spain, welcomed Haller's critique with enthusiasm.

When the Spanish chargé d'affaires at Vienna protested against the appearance of the book, Metternich brusquely dismissed him. For his part, Hardenberg believed himself obliged to state that "Haller's work is better than a good piece of literature; it offers a good treatment," and he charged Arnim with not hiding from the people of Berne "in what high esteem the author was held by the better sort."[38]

It was at that time, the Swiss historian Oechsli tells us, that at the Prussian court they thought seriously of having the "great Berner", as they pointedly called him, come to Berlin.

Doubtlessly Hegel would be able to evaluate the sincerity of the good wishes Hardenberg addressed to Haller, a man whose opinions ran in general so directly counter to those of the chancellor.

Nevertheless Hegel treated Haller quite harshly in his *Philosophy of Right*, denouncing his "lack of thought" [*Gedankenlosigkeit*],[39] his "hatred of all laws", his "flabby-mindedness", his "hypocrisy".[40] Hegel exposed the contradictions in Haller's ideas, and was not sparing of their author.

Did he not risk thereby unleashing on himself the anger of the courtiers and their servile writers, that of the crown prince, that of the king perhaps, and (who knows?) the resentment of Metternich himself? And especially so, after they had put on the other side of the balance to his attack on Haller his thin criticisms of Rousseau and his ambiguous outburst against Fries?

We can only imagine the unpleasantness that might have overwhelmed Hegel in this eventuality. In fact it did not come to pass. A surprising revelation, which came to light between the time when Hegel wrote the *Philosophy of Right* (1820) and the time when, due to the slowness of the censors, it appeared, temporarily took away from Haller's friends any possibility of action.

It is difficult to believe that Hegel would have heard as early as 1820 the rumour that was confidentially whispered in certain circles: Haller was said to have rejected Protestantism and gone over to Catholicism!

Even so it was nothing more than an unconfirmed rumour, one that Haller's friends and disciples quickly denounced as a vile calumny, made up out of whole cloth by subversive minds. Had not Haller, as the law required, solemnly confessed the Lutheran religion on becoming a member of the Grand Council of Berne?

At the moment of composing the venomous note in the *Philosophy of Right*, Hegel could not have known Haller to be an apostate.   Perhaps, however, unreliable rumour or exceptional flair led him to suspect Haller's "hypocrisy".

But by 1821, when Hegel's work appeared, Haller's situation had radically changed. To the great distress of his Prussian disciples, there had appeared simultaneously in French and in German, at Metz and Strassburg, a pamphlet that would go through numerous editions and would soon receive a preface by De Bonald: the *Letter of Mr. Carl Ludwig Haller to his family in explanation of his return to the Catholic church.*

Haller publicly acknowledged that "since the year 1808 he had been Catholic in spirit and Protestant only in name,"[41] and he claimed that "the revolution of the 16th century that we call the Reformation is, in its principle, means and results, the perfect image and precursor of the political revolution of our time." His antipathy for the latter had made him "disgusted with the former."[42]

This confession provoked a scandal in Protestant countries and thereby rendered unintentional aid to the cause of progress. The most celebrated theoretician of the Restoration in the Protestant countries had removed his mask: showing himself to be a liar who, though Catholic, had yet maintained for some time a facade of Protestantism for the better propagation of his philosophy in German language countries.[43]

The adversaries of Catholicism saw their thesis confirmed, according to which that religion served as a prop of reaction. Even more, the adversaries of reaction noted its partiality for Catholicism.

Strangely enough, the political justification that Haller offered for his repudiation corresponded exactly with Hegel's increasingly profound conviction: Haller condemned the Reformation because, according to him, it had paved the way for the Revolution in that it encouraged free thought and instituted a religion of freedom. For the same reasons, Hegel on the contrary approved of the Reformation and considered it to be a key event in the history of the emancipation of the human spirit.

Convicted of perjury, Haller was excluded from the Grand Council of Berne; and this time the Prussian envoy was unable to intervene in his favour. He emigrated to Paris, where the "ultras" welcomed him warmly, and where he collaborated with them.

Protestant clergymen and professors pronounced their most severe censure on the apostate. Many of his former admirers turned against him. The reactionaries who remained faithful found themselves constrained to be silent for the moment; they dared not reply publicly to progressives like Hegel, who attacked him.

The man of influence, heeded and admired, whose theories Hegel dared to criticize, had in the interim become someone impossible to defend in Berlin.

Willy-nilly, the reactionaries abandoned the deserter to public contempt; although retaining his ideas – they are to be found almost verbatim in the text of Frederick William IV cited above[44] – they looked around for another flag-bearer.

They then turned to Savigny (1779-1861)*, the leader of the "school of historical law," who explicitly developed his ideas in reaction to those of Hegel's friend, the jurist Thibaut, of Heidelberg. In 1814 the latter published a study *On the necessity of a universal civil law for Germany* in which he expressed the national need for a unified, coherent and codified legal system. One detects the influence of a great example – that of Napoleon's civil code. At the time Hegel made common cause with Thibaut.[45]

Savigny set himself against this theory in his book, *On the call of our time for legislation and a legal science* (1814), in which he challenged the usefulness and indeed the legitimacy of attempts to reform the established law in any age whatever. Genuine law rests on tradition and develops in an "organic' manner. One must neither disturb it, nor modify it, nor even codify it.

Savigny fought against every attempt to introduce French civil law into Germany, as well as every effort to unify German law. He thus supported the separatism of the small German states, and contributed to maintaining the juridicial retardation of Germany.

We can see that the Prussian reaction occasionally changed its ideologues. But one could always be found. In any case, it could also turn to France for advice.

But as for Hegel and his friends, both German and French, they were not found in that camp.

NOTES

1. See W. Bauer, *Prinzess Wilhelmina von Preussen, geborene Marianne von Hessen-Homburg* (Homburg, 1886) 45.

2. *Briefe* III, 472, note of Hoffmeister.

3. *Philosophy of Right* #280, Addition.

4. See Rosenzweig, *Hegel und der Staat* (Berlin & Munich, 1920) ii, 141.

5. *Briefe* III, 136; *Letters*, 645.

6. Roques, *op.cit.* 351.

7. K. Varnhagen von Ense, *Blätter aus der preussischen Geschichte*, ed. L. Assing (Leipzig, 1868) IV, 127.

8. *Briefe* III, 182; See *Letters*, 646f.

9. This on account of an article in the *Constitutionnel* which praised Hegel's behaviour with respect to Cousin. (See *Briefe* III, notes to pp 377-78.) Knowledge of all these facts allows a greater appreciation of the nuances of Hegel's speech in honour of the tercentenary of the Augsburg Confession, given on June 21, 1830: "The piety of our princes thus gives us a solid foundation for untroubled confidence and establishes a bond of affection between them and us. If every year on the birthday of our gracious king, Frederick William, we lift our eyes to him and meditate on his benefactions, which he has allowed this university to receive in such rich measure, so today we want joyfully to celebrate his exalted piety, the source of all virtues." (Hegel, *Berliner Schriften*, 55.)

10. See the long note to Paragraph 258.

11. *Philosophy of Right*, # 281, Addition (p.289).

12. Texts of Frederick William IV, cited from A. Cornu, *op.cit.* 168.

13. F. Ancillon, *Ueber Souveränität und Staatsverfassung* (Berlin, 1816) 3.

14. G.W.F. Hegel, *Early Theological Writings* (tr. Knox and Kröner) (New York, 1961) 80; see also in *Hegel's theologische Jugendschriften*, ed. Nohl (Tübingen, 1907) 45.

15. G.W.F. Hegel, *The Philosophy of History*, tr. Sibree (New York, 1956) 23.

16. See Ibid. 104, and also 139.

17. Ibid. 437f.

18. G.W.F. Hegel, *Lectures on the History of Philosophy*, (London, 1895) III, 391.

19. See A. Cornu, *op.cit.* 173 and note 4.

20. Marginal notes in Hegel's own handwriting, in G.W.F. Hegel, *Grundlinien der Philosophie des Rechts*, ed. Hoffmeister (Meiner, 1955) 354.

21. *Briefe* II, 279; *Letters*, 463.

22. F. Engels, "Revolution and Counter-revolution in Germany," in Marx-Engels, *Collected Works* XI (New York, 1978) 21.

23. See *Neue Deutsche Biographie* I (Berlin, 1952) 264-5.

24. *Ueber Souveränität und Staatsverfassungen.* The work remained in print for a long time. One finds it announced in 1833 just after Volume VII of Hegel's *Works* as appearing from the same publishing house.

25. *op.cit.* 1.

26. Ibid. 47.

27. See above p. 69

28. *op. cit.* 35.

29. Ibid. 72.

30. Ibid. 76, 93.

31. Ibid. 54-55.

32. Ibid. 102.

33. *Restauration der Staatswissenschaften*, I (1816), II (1817), III (1818), IV (1820), etc.

34. Cited by W. Oechsli, *Geschichte der Schweiz im Neunzehnten Jahrhundert* (Leipzig, 1903-1913) II, 541.

35. Hegel severely criticized the inquisition in a note on Galileo. (*Philosophy of Right* #270.)

36. See K. Obermann, *Deutschland 1815-1849* (Berlin, 1961) 39.

37. Oechsli, *op.cit.* II, 542.

38. Oechsli, ibid.

39. *Philosophy of Right*, #219.

40. Ibid. # 258n.

41. C.L. Haller, *Lettre de M. Charles Louis de Haller à sa famille, pour lui déclarer son retour à l'église catholique, apostolique et romaine* (Metz, 1821) 7.

42. Ibid. 8.

43. Ibid. 9: "I had hoped that my fourth volume would have more influence in seeming to come from the pen of a Protestant."

44. See above pp. 68-9.

45. Roques, *op.cit.* 256.

Part Two

The 'Demagogues'

I

The Attack

1. Fries

Without any doubt, if Hegel was considered for so long to be a complaisant servant of the powers that be, it was because of the Fries affair.

In essence, he owes his bad reputation to several lines from the Preface to the *Philosophy of Right* in which he handled this individual rather roughly. The diatribe against Fries gives to the preface the air of a vicious polemic; it is rude, unpolished and disagreeable. It contributes little to Hegel's standing.

Nevertheless the importance of this passage is exaggerated; and any interpretation which concentrates on discovering there some clue to Hegel's political orientation is one-sided.

Here is what Hegel published:

A ringleader of these hosts of superficiality, of these self-styled 'philosophers', Herr Fries, did not blush, on the occasion of a public festival which has become notorious, to express the following ideas in a speech on 'The state and the constitution': 'In the people ruled by a genuine communal spirit, life for the discharge of all public business would come from below, from the people itself; living associations, indissolubly united by the holy chain of friendship, would be dedicated to every single project of popular education and popular service', and so on. This is the quintessence of shallow thinking, to base philosophic science not on the development of thought and the concept but on immediate sense-perception and the play of fancy; to take the rich inward articulation of ethical life, i.e. the state, the architectonic of that life's rationality, ... to take this structure and confound the completed fabric in the broth of 'heart, friendship, and inspiration'. According to a view of this kind, the world of ethics ... should be given over – as in fact of course it is not – to the subjective

> ascribing to feeling the labour, the more than millennary labour, of reason and its intellect, all the trouble of rational insight and knowledge directed by speculative thinking is of course saved....[1]

Hegel then alluded to the Mephistopheles of Goethe who charges minds with bringing ruin on themselves whenever they disdain understanding and knowledge. In this way he gave expression to his antipathy for the philosophy of sentiment and intuition. Here there is nothing really novel with respect to his thought.

What was novel was Fries' situation at the very moment when he was subjected to this disdainful criticism. Had not Hegel directed this rebuke at the very words which were declaimed during the famous demonstration at Wartburg?*

It had been organized by the students' association, the *Burschenschaft*; and several incidents that took place there gave the reactionary authorities a pretext for taking all kinds of repressive measures against this patriotic and semi-liberal movement.

By criticizing Fries on this occasion Hegel would seem to be associating himself with the government action, and to be participating directly in the struggle of the reactionaries against the German progressives; it would seem particularly so for those readers who do not know of the two philosophers' previous quarrels.

But when examined more calmly and within its context, "the Fries affair" does not justify this first impression. Even less does it justify the generalizations which have relied on it for support. Was it not by thinking of Fries in particular that Flint was led to formulate this severe condemnation?

> Hegel practiced conservatism and conformism; he denounced liberals and reformers; he put his trust in the reactionary government."[2]

Let us imagine a *Philosophy of Right* where this unfortunate passage about Fries did not figure. The accusation of reaction and servility would then lose its principal justification.

But this justification itself lacks consistency. Let us describe the public and personal circumstances of this incident. It will enable us to correct the simplistic schema in which a generous and persecuted liberal on one side confronts on the other a lackey of the powers that be, one sufficiently debased to strike an opponent already victim of repression.

This cliché misrepresents the facts. We certainly do not want to disparage the merit of Fries, particularly at a time when gestures of opposition remained so uncommon and tentative. But we cannot allow the attribution of qualities he did not possess and opinions that were not his own simply to highlight Hegel's mistake.

2. The perennial rival

To understand Hegel's behaviour, unsatisfactory though it be, we have to remember that the two men had known each other for a long time, and that an ongoing quarrel tied them one to another. In that light, the blow that Hegel threw at Fries in 1821 appears as simply one episode among many others, one of the sparring sessions of the match.

They had met twenty years earlier at Jena. Fries was then completing his studies in the town to which the older Hegel came to establish himself after a long apprenticeship as tutor in Switzerland and Frankfurt. They both acquired the doctoral degree in 1801.

The competition between them soon saw the light of day, for together they became "private instructors" (*Privatdozent*). It seems that Fries taught without much success.

Each *Privatdozent* strove to be named as quickly as possible, first to the post of "extraordinary professor", and then to that of "ordinary professor". Even as early as 1804 Hegel was afraid that he would lose out to his competitors, and in particular to Fries.

So he ventured to forward directly to the minister, Goethe, a letter in which he tacitly protested against a favoritism which threatened him. Since the style of this letter, with its incredible stodginess, must have made quite a bad impression on its recipient, it does not serve to dispel the sense of some conscious embarrassment. One cannot translate it without lightening it somewhat. Here is what Goethe could read there, among other things:

> Since I hear that a few of my colleagues expect to be graciously appointed to professorships in philosophy, and since I am thus reminded that I am the oldest *Privatdozent* in philosophy locally, I venture to put it to Your Excellency to decide whether I must not fear being held back from working at the university according to my abilities, should the high authorities grant such a distinction to others.[3]

Perhaps this ponderous intervention allowed Hegel to avoid something worse. The delay in his career when compared with that of the younger Fries could not be undone — an incurable wound in self-esteem for Hegel, who despised his colleague. At least both of them became "extraordinary professors" at the same time in 1805: a post called extraordinary by virtue of its mediocrity, but nevertheless the antechamber to a full professorship.

Hegel already had the impression that the authorities were partial to Fries, and on that account he felt some resentment. In addition, and in particular, the theory Fries expounded combined Hegel's two philosophical enemies: Kantianism and sentimentalism. What was there to nourish a strong friendship?

The animosity was soon intensified. Hardly had Fries obtained the status of "extraordinary professor" at Jena than, in the same year, he succeeded in obtaining a post as professor at the university of Heidelberg. With that he blithely entered on a university career. Hegel was left to vegetate for a long time, and only eleven years later benefit from a similar promotion. Only in 1816 would he fully enter academia — also at Heidelberg.

The evidence that he received of Fries's incompetence increased his bitterness. A former student of Hegel, who later lived in Heidelberg and thus could compare the two rivals, wrote to him:

> Fries has little success; he is too ponderous! I attended his lectures sometimes, but his manner is so wearying that one falls asleep.[4]

Other witnesses as well attest to the failure of Fries's instruction at Heidelberg.[5]

Several years later, in 1811, Fries published in this town a *System of Logic*. Once again Hegel lagged behind his junior.

He lacked sufficient leisure since he had to earn his living in an occupation alien to the properly philosophic task. His *Science of Logic* appeared only in 1812. Fries's book had the benefit of priority in the eyes of the public, and, since one does not usually buy or read a treatise on logic every year, Hegel's work certainly suffered as a result.

From 1811 on Hegel applied to Fries's *Logic* extremely severe criticisms. It is useful to recall them to remind ourselves of their tone. They at times surpass in harshness those which Hegel expressed ten years later in the *Philosophy of Right*. So it is not Fries's attitude at the *Wartburg* nor the influence of the "Prussian spirit" that explains the cruel formulas of the *Philosophy of Right*.

In a letter of 1811 Hegel confided to Niethammer his opinion of Fries's work. It is almost impossible to express in English these ponderous sentences, in which Hegel's disdain and hatred of Fries breathes like a noxious vapour. Let us try all the same to offer a characteristic fragment:

> Heidelberg, however, brings me to Fries and his *Logic*. ... My feeling in connection with it is one of sadness. I do not know whether as a married man I am mellowing, but I feel sadness that in the name of philosophy such a shallow man attains the honorable position he holds in the world, and that he even permits himself to inject such scribblings with an air of importance. On such occasions one can become angry that there is no public voice to speak with integrity in such matters, for certain circles and persons would greatly benefit from it. I have known this Fries for a long time. I know that he has gone beyond the Kantian philosophy by interpreting it in the most superficial manner, by earnestly watering it down ever more, making it ever more shallow. The paragraphs of his *Logic* and the accompanying explanations are printed in separate volumes. The first volume of paragraphs is spiritless, completely shallow, threadbare, trivial, devoid of the least intimation of scientific coherence. The explanations are [likewise] totally shallow, devoid of spirit, threadbare, trivial, the most slovenly disconnected explanatory lecture-hall twaddle, such as only a truly empty-headed individual in his hour of digestion could ever come up with.[6]

Bitter rancor serves to render Hegel's style more ponderous still.

If several readers in 1821 were amazed and angered by the ill-humour Hegel poured out on Fries, Niethammer, at least, should have experienced no surprise. In the 1811 letter from which we have just cited, Hegel savaged Fries for more than a page, and with spleen!

Without experiencing much relief, for all that. For even in his *Science of Logic* he could not refrain from venting his opinion of Fries once again, this time publicly. A note was devoted to him — a note that in due course would cause headaches:

> The latest treatment of this science which has recently appeared, *System of Logic* by Fries, returns to the anthropological foundations. The idea or opinion on which it is based is so shallow, both in itself and in its execution, that I am spared the trouble of taking any notice of this insignificant publication.[7]

One can easily imagine that such words would incite Fries's wrath, (as Paulus informed Hegel).[8] Hegel's friends, including Paulus himself, did not have the same motives for turning against Fries. They did not understand this quarrel; none of them rose to a level of competence sufficient to appreciate objectively the motives for Hegel's anger, which appeared excessive to them. The note in the *Science of Logic* provoked some unhappiness, and even irritation, among the philosopher's associates.

On account of this note the *Heidelberger Jahrbücher*, which Paulus edited and in which Fries collaborated, did not publish a review of the *Science of Logic*. Fries began by remaining silent for a long time — an effective way of showing in turn his disdain. Then, two years after it appeared, he wrote an article in which he reviewed Hegel's volume at the same time as the works of Bouterwek, E.-G. Schulze and Herbart. To the clarity of these latter works he opposed the "shadows of the [Hegelian] speculative philosophy".

He described Hegel's logic as "a metaphysics according to the dogmatic method", "a new dogmatic exposition of ontology". Its author

> does not understand himself, does not take account of the fact that he has himself published a phenomenology of spirit using a psychological approach.[9]

Hegel's admirers were furious, and he himself was even more so. Van Ghert wrote: "I saw the miserable review of your *Logic* by Fries. I had not known that he was so mean."[10]

Hegel's note, his attacks on Fries, and the latter's response, all did little to favour Hegel's appointment to Heidelberg, an appointment long wished for, but officially proposed only in 1816.

When it finally arrived, however, it was once again under quite humiliating conditions. In effect, to get a post at Heidelberg, Hegel had to wait until Fries had abandoned it by accepting an invitation from Jena. Hegel had to be content with what Fries had left behind.

From the time of his first lectures at Heidelberg, Hegel lamented at length the platitudes to which German philosophy had descended in the preceding years. Without naming him, he clearly had Fries in mind:

> [Due to] the needs of the time ... it has thus happened that, because vigorous natures turned to the practical,[11] insipidity and dullness appropriated to themselves the pre-eminence in Philosophy, and flourished there. It may indeed be said that since philosophy began to take a place in Germany, it has never looked so badly as at the present time — never have emptiness and shallowness overlaid it so completely, and never have they spoken and acted with such arrogance, as though all power were in their hands![12]

However, Hegel was not finished with Fries. When the question of his appointment at Berlin arose, he came up against his perennial rival once more. It would not have needed very much for Fries's friends in Berlin to have scuppered Hegel's candidacy. At the very least, in 1816 they helped to delay the decision.

Jena, Heidelberg and Berlin: each time that the hope of a better and more respectable situation was offered to Hegel, Fries's shadow arrived to take it away, or to tarnish it. And each time it infuriated Hegel.

In his teaching at Heidelberg he provided proof of his professional superiority to Fries. Nor was he reluctant to express his self-satisfaction, while disparaging his opponent. In a letter of 1817 he wrote:

> Interest in philosophy that Fries had all but allowed to die out— at least assuming my syntax passes muster here— nonetheless seems still to have been actual. In logic, where he had five to six students, I have about seventy this semester. And I prefer to have them in my second rather than first semester.[13]

Now the addressee of that letter, the bookseller Frommann, lived in Jena where Fries was currently teaching, and was on friendly terms with him. In this situation, how can we fail to sense Hegel's mischievous purpose: the desire to harm Fries's reputation and career?

The philosophical conflict between Hegel and Fries developed at the same time as their professional rivalry. For some time it had concerned epistemology, logic and metaphysics. It extended even to the realm of science. In 1822 Fries published his *Mathematical Philosophy of Nature, developed according to the philosophic method*. It took its stand quite far from the Hegelian options. Hegel's student, Hinrichs, accused it of having a fault meriting a refund: it removed everything qualitative from nature.[14]

The conflict between Hegel and Fries even acquired force from their thought, and one is led to ask oneself if, in some instances, the choice of the one cannot be explained, at least in part, by the inverse choice of the other. Fries parodied Goethe's theory of colour which, in contrast, Hegel defended with vigor.

3. Fries's "Liberalism"

There is nothing surprising in the fact that Hegel, in the Preface to the *Philosophy of Right*, condemned anew the "subjectivity", the "sentimentalism" and the "platitudes" of Fries's opinions. These had just been spread out to view once again in the *Wartburg* speech.

To put it simply, those who do not know about the long quarrel may be surprised by the bitterness of tone. But they also risk not taking enough notice enough of the fact that Hegel was really taking a philosophical position: he had Fries's political stance less in mind than the subjectivist way of justifying it. He did not directly condemn the *Wartburg* as such. He took on Fries, and not the other speakers, whom he nevertheless knew quite well; some of them, like Oken and Carové, were among his friends.

However, what has provoked indignation is the significance Hegel's diatribe assumed, whether intentionally or not, in the circumstances of its appearance.

After 1816 Fries's image acquired a new dimension. The patriotic association of students, the *Burschenschaft*, regarded him as one of its spiritual heroes; this choice already lets us see the ideological shortcomings of this movement, progressive though it was in some of its aspects. Hegel's text does not specify sufficiently clearly that Fries was criticised as spokesman for subjectivism, and not as spokesman for the political opposition.

The speech that Fries made at the *Wartburg*, which provoked Hegel's new explosion of anger, was not at all as "revolutionary" and as "liberal" as one is led to believe from hearing of the traditional opposition between a Fries "of the left" and a Hegel "of the right". His words tended rather towards appeasement and conciliation; and Hegel, from the point of view which interested him, judged them impartially. They were particularly remarkable for their insignificance, for the absence of any clear political thought in them, for their effective "banality". Fries had abandoned himself to sentimental phraseology.[15]

What was somewhat revolutionary was Fries's *participation* in the demonstration: not the content of his speech, but the fact that he had made it. This involvement attracted the attention of the reactionaries, frightened to learn of the progress of a patriotic movement slightly touched with liberalism. Metternich became anxious; the Prussian government applied pressure on that of Saxe-Weimar, which was responsible for Jena.

At the request of the "Commission of Mainz", charged by the Holy Alliance with the task of suppressing liberal "intrigues", and at Hardenberg's instigation, the government of Saxe-Weimar agreed in 1817 to suspend Fries from his academic duties.

In his Preface Hegel took issue publicly with a victim of counter-revolutionary repression, and dealt him further blows.

That provoked the well-known protest of the *Halleschen Allgemeinen Literaturzeitung*, which stressed this point in an article:

> From what we know, Mr. Fries has had no happy lot, and the author's behaviour to him is like the scorning and intentional insulting of an already afflicted man. Such conduct is *noble in no way*, but the reviewer will not call it by the name which it deserves, leaving the choice to the reflective reader.[16]

Hegel, who took this rebuke badly, was furious; in his anger he went to the point of asking for sanctions from Altenstein against a journal which put in question the rectitude of his behaviour. Although badly understood to be sure, he yet saw himself slandered by the "subjectivist sect". To achieve justice for himself, he did not hesitate to boast of his quality as an official; and he criticised once again "this party which thinks itself privileged, and is used to assume inflated importance" because it abuses an "over-extensive freedom of the press".[17]

Altenstein administered a severe warning to the journal, but wisely refrained from taking more serious measures, suggesting that Hegel apply to the courts if he really believed himself subject to criminal libel.

What are we to think of Hegel's behaviour in this whole affair? It certainly does not present the most attractive side of his personality. Hegel had abandoned himself to a way of evening scores. He did not want to let pass an occasion for taking revenge for humiliations, of which Fries had been more the instrument than the instigator.

Rosenkranz holds that, in the Preface, Hegel did not intend to attack Fries personally. But how can we believe that? Up to this point Hegel had never been able to speak of him without piling on sarcasm.

Far reaching sarcasm! Only because of it has posterity retained in its memory the name of Fries, ironically confirming Hegel's judgement a century and a half after the event. Hegel's genius infinitely surpassed that of Fries. By preferring the latter, the academic authorities and a part of the public treated Hegel with the ultimate injustice — an injustice that Altenstein redressed at last by inviting the philosopher to Berlin.

It is precisely this final and brilliant restitution that leads us to condemn Hegel's attitude in 1821. In the last analysis he had triumphed. He now saw himself "recognized", as he liked to say. Why not throw away the old animosity? Why not keep silent about Fries? Victorious, did Hegel have to lower himself by hitting his opponent when he was down?

Let us recognize this lack of tact, if nothing more. Hegel's character bore this trait of meanness.

Nevertheless we do not have to confer on this affair a significance that is in fact foreign to it. The incident arose from Hegel's private revenge both against a man, and against a philosophical current, one which was in danger of "subverting" a political current.

One can resist this philosophy and its attempts at appropriation without thereby radically challenging the politics it wants to influence. If Hegel was really less "democratic" than Fries — and that could be contested — that does not amount to much. Victor Cousin, at the time of his first visit to Germany, could discern between them but very little difference from the political point of view.

Cousin was sympathetic with the "liberalism" of Fries, who in conversation declared himself in favour of the approach of Royer-Collard.[18] But he discovered almost the same opinions with Hegel:

> So he was sincerely constitutional and openly declared himself for the cause that Mr. Royer-Collard supported and represented in France. He spoke to me of our affairs as did Mr. Fries at Jena, with less liveliness and enthusiasm to be sure, but with deep feeling.[19]

Even though the conflict between Hegel and Fries was not based primarily on political motives, Hegel's Preface did not display the character of a denunciation; nor did it imply approval of the sanctions taken against Fries. Solemnly and publicly Fries had spoken the words that Hegel reproduced. His "suspension" lay well in the past.

But we have to make clear that the persecution of Fries remained nothing more than a matter of principle. The Duke of Weimar suspended him from his duties only reluctantly, and he did so in order to obey, at least for appearances' sake, the orders of the Commission of Mainz. In reality Fries retained a very comfortable position. In high places they did not cease treating him with respect; they kept on paying his salary; and they even authorized him to continue his teaching *in private*, whenever he did not prefer to travel.

Invidious though the sanctions taken against him were, they nevertheless did not make him into a pitiable victim. Many other men suffered a much more brutal repression, particularly in Prussia, and, as we shall see, Hegel did not abandon them; he energetically defended them and offered them aid.

It seems to us that Hegel had had the particular intention of making the members of the *Burschenschaft* wary of a false and dangerous philosophical approach. It cannot be ruled out of court that Hegel had in mind a confrontation with Fries with respect to the ideological inspiration of the thoroughly divided *Burschenschaft*. Many of its members, and among them the most prominent, preferred Hegel to Fries: for example Carové, founder of the "*Allgemeinen Burschenschaft*", Griesheim,[20] Asverus[21] and, most typically, Förster, a former disciple of Fries, who joined the Hegelian camp to become Hegel's student as well as his friend.[22]

In the Preface to the *Philosophy of Right* we discover Hegel's aversion to liberalism, to "abstract democracy", to "individualistic atomism"; and that leads us to picture his adversary as a champion of liberalism in the sense that we understand the term in our day.

Now, in the Prussia of 1820, the fundamental political battle was between the nobility and the middle class. Which would be successful: feudalism or capitalism? Liberalism and democracy were without doubt the most typical means for achieving a victory of the middle class in general. But frequently they were nothing more than a mere veil, behind which the effective dictatorship of the middle class could, albeit with difficulty, hide itself. Hegel would not have had questions about this. He had taken his stand against feudalism.

Within the liberal camp he criticised more the use of certain methods than the ends desired. We can assume that his disagreements with the liberals were subordinate to a shared goal: the achieving of political power by the middle class and its officials. And Hegel had a clearer perception of this goal than many of the declared and accredited liberals.

Nevertheless Hegel did not reject liberalism completely in all its aspects; on the contrary he retained a good many liberal principles in his own political ideas. If he did not confuse political progress with the extension of liberalism, he still did not exclude from his theory all liberal features.

On the other hand, the German "liberals" of his time were to be found much more "to the right" than we are at first inclined to suppose. Much more hesitant than that of their French contemporaries, their "liberalism" allowed for strange impurities.

Fries can indeed be seen as a symbol of the extreme confusion which at that time characterized this political movement. There was nothing more eclectic and more vague than the content of his speeches, which, unfortunately, gained some precision and focus only when he let himself loose into chauvinism, xenophobia and antisemitism. One faction of the *Burschenschaft* accompanied him on this path. Quite clearly Hegel could not do so, and he was not the only one to condemn these follies.

A single anecdote will provide us with proof that other distinguished men noticed Fries's weakness.

In 1814 the *Heidelberger Jahrbücher* published an article on the theory of colours. Goethe's position was treated with contempt, and Hegel was accused of having adopted it.

In 1816 Goethe asked his friend, Boisserée, the well-known art collector, about the person who had written the article. This is Boisserée's response, dated 1817:

> The review is by the philosopher Fries who, because he has not been successful in philosophy, has plunged into astronomy for women, then into a physics of resources, and now into the hatred of Jews and into Teutonism, all for the sake of buttering his bread.... The shallow drivel of Fries, which arrogates to itself here and there a hypocritical love of science, has had a quite unfortunate influence among all who are ingenuous.[23]

Fries had a number of enemies other than Hegel who could not forgive him for advocating teutonism and antisemitism in the *Burschenschaft*, which was much too disposed to welcome them.

The indecision and the inconsistency of Fries's political opinions becomes clear in the justification he offered for his position twenty years later. He would dissociate himself from those who had listened to him in 1817 and from the *Burschenschaft*. He would deny that he then had the political tendencies which people now want to ascribe to him as a sign of merit, and which are supposed to have provoked Hegel's hostility.

In his old age he would declare that he had had no revolutionary intentions, and that his success with the students,

> in reality carried no scientific meaning, for only the political allusions attracted attention; my philosophical and scientific interests attracted none at all; and [he added to put himself in a good light] my exhortations to undertake studies in political science instead of becoming charlatans were noticed only by a very few.

But was it not that Fries's speech had limited itself to "exhorting" undertaking scientific studies? Hegel accused him of not himself proceeding to scientific studies, and of then constructing his conception of the state without basing it on a solid foundation. Fries was not far from retrospectively acknowledging that his ventures had been understood by his disciples, who approved of them, in the same terms as they had been by Hegel, who condemned them.

Fries offered this further commentary on his former opinions:

> When I spoke so zealously against the Jewish community as a pernicious social growth within the German cultural life ... people said of me that I hated the Jews and advocated their destruction. But I was advocating that the Jewish community be reformed and dissolved as a commercial caste, so that the Jews could enter the state as fully qualified citizens, no longer making illegal profits from their neighbours.[24]

We can see, twenty years after the *Wartburg*, that Fries would not succeed very well in clarifying his ideas. In the same breath as he belatedly defended himself from ever being an antisemite, he remained a prisoner of prejudice against the Jewish "commercial caste" and its "illegitimate privileges".

All in all, Hegel's attitude to Fries, although unfortunate in human terms, does not seem to us particularly reactionary. To the personal enmity is connected a theoretical disagreement: rationalism against confused sentimentalism.

Hegel threw himself on his adversary without second thoughts and without any calculation. Despite all his weaknesses and mistakes, Fries represented one current of opposition to absolutism. His philosophy was perhaps regressive, but in a single person political attitudes do not always correspond to philosophical choices.

In certain circumstances, is it appropriate to put a damper on philosophical quarrels to achieve a political common ground, albeit partial and ephemeral? That is a question of tactics. But in a work like the *Philosophy of Right*, that wanted to be strictly scientific, tactical precautions would have led to theoretical compromise.

Hegel was developing a rationalist conception of the state. From this perspective, sentimentalism was the enemy. Hegel attacked it with all the greater vigour because it found embodiment in a detested adversary.

But he did not thereby agree to being classified among the reactionaries. Remarking to his friend Daub on the repercussions of the attack on Fries and his "barren and pretentious sect" and noting that some had taken umbrage at the attack, Hegel added:

> They could not blame what I said on what was previously called the "Schmalz group"[25] and therefore were all the more at a loss as to how to categorize it.[26]

It is easy to understand why Hegel had criticized Fries. But in the manner of doing so had he not surrendered to secondary tactical considerations? As part of the Preface, the tirade against Fries opens the *Philosophy of Right* and seems to put the whole work under its inspiration, while the virulent criticism of Haller takes refuge primarily in a note, quite long to be sure, but buried in the depths of the text.

In an aphorism from the Jena period, Hegel had said:

The royal road in philosophy usually consists in reading the prefaces and reviews, in order to acquire an approximate representation of the subject.[27]

The key people in a monarchy certainly use the royal road. The courtiers and the feudal class, if they read at all, will read little else than the prefaces. The royal censors doubtless will not go much further, at least if it is a question of comprehension.

Against the threats of censorship and of the police, the "anti-Friesianism" of the Preface would, in the last analysis, have served as a lightning conductor for the whole *Philosophy of Right*.

NOTES

1. *Hegel's Philosophy of Right*, 5-6.

2. Flint, *op.cit.* 136.

3. *Briefe*, I, 84; *Letters*, 685.

4. *Briefe*, I, 105.

5. See *Allgemeine Deutsche Biographie*, "Fries", 75.

6. *Briefe* I, 338f; Letters, 257.

7. *Hegel's Science of Logic*, tr. Miller, 52n.

8. *Briefe* II, 32, and 41-42.

9. Cited in *Briefe* II, 381-2, notes by Hoffmeister.

10. *Briefe* II, 136.

11. During this period Hegel had successively edited a newspaper in Bamberg, and been in charge of a high school in Nürnberg.

12. "Inaugural Address delivered at Heidelberg on the 28th October, 1816," in *Hegel's Lectures on the History of Philosophy*, tr. E.S. Haldane, (London, 1892) I, xii.

13. *Briefe* II, 154; *Letters,* 434.

14. *Briefe* II, 300.

15. The text of this speech can be found in a pamphlet of F.J. Frommann (the son of Hegel's friend): *Das Burschenfest auf der Wartburg, 18./19. Oktober 1817,* Jena 1818, p. 19.

16. See Hegel, *Berliner Schriften,* 750-751. [also K. Rosenkranz, *G.W.F. Hegels Leben,* 336.]

17. Ibid. [Rosenkranz, p. 337.]

18. V. Cousin, *Souvenirs d'Allemagne, Revue des deux mondes*, August 1866, 606.

19. Ibid. 617.

20. *Briefe* II, 482.

21. Ibid. 435. See *Letters*, 447ff.

22. Ibid. 471. See *Letters*, 446f.

23. *Briefe* II, 418. Cited by Hoffmeister.

24. Fries's claims are cited by Hoffmeister, *Briefe* II, 444-445.

25. The reactionary jurist, Schmalz, had attracted the hatred of the members of the *Burschenschaft*; at the festival of the *Wartburg*, for example, they had cried; "Down with the Schmalz group." (See F.J. Frommann, *op.cit.* 24-25.) Hegel did not want to be classified among the enemies of the *Burschenschaft*.

26. *Briefe* II, 263; *Letters*, 461.

27. *Dokumente zu Hegels Entwicklung,* 369.

II

The "Burschenschaft"

1. Its Merits

There were positions to be taken other than those of Fries or of the reaction. In fact, quite diverse tendencies quarrelled among themselves within the *Burschenschaft*, while others were grouped around its fringes. Incoherent and frequently eccentric, the whole lot did not represent a very powerful force. But the monarchy and the feudal class were still frightened by the memory of the French Revolution and watched with apprehension the agitation, childish though it frequently was, of all the "demagogues".

The origin of the patriotic student associations is well known.

A great number of teachers and students had participated as volunteers in the 1813 and 1815 wars of national liberation. Inspired by a sincere patriotism, they sought the unification of their country as well as its political regeneration in a more democratic form.

During those difficult years, the king of Prussia and several other sovereigns promised them that constitutions would be granted; on their return from the war they waited impatiently for the fulfilment of these promises. They were in no way calling for the destruction of the monarchy and the institution of a republic; all they sought was a weakening of absolutism.

On the whole their demands remained quite moderate, as was the case with the whole liberal movement in Europe between 1820 and 1830 – even in France, where it proved to be less daring than we sometimes suppose nowadays.

Here is how Ponteil presents the European liberalism of 1815:

> Everywhere the liberals engaged in violent struggles against the old autocracy and aristocracy, attempting to establish a constitutional system based on the upper middle classes, that is to say, primarily on the bourgeoisie that is rich enough to be able to reflect and think.[1]

This "bourgeoisie that is rich enough to be able to reflect and think" bears obvious similarities to the governing class of the state as conceived by Hegel in the *Philosophy of Right*.

In making more precise the goals which it sought, F. Ponteil added:

> From a political point of view, the liberalism of 1815 proposed to limit the despotism of the sovereign and of the administration, to have included within a written constitution the recognition of personal freedom, the freedom of speech, of the press, of assembly and of association. The common idea in this constitutional movement was that all authority, whether monarchical or of the people, ought to be limited. Nevertheless liberal conceptions varied. The moderate ones satisfied themselves with limited suffrage. The governing of a country belongs to an elite. Power must rest in the elements of stability and order, that is, in those people who, provided with stable property, regularly receive income and pay taxes: this is a system of government based on property.[2]

Nothing in that goes much further than Hegel's *Philosophy of Right*, although occasionally it arrives at the same conclusions by other means.

At the forefront of this movement, French liberalism did not manifest an audacity that was noticeably more revolutionary. Mme de Staël took a stand against royal absolutism, but also against "revolutionary despotism", which "one saw coming from the meanest classes of society like vapours rising from a pestilent swamp." She declared herself in favour of "independent intermediary political bodies". Like Benjamin Constant,* she preferred a hereditary monarchy because "an elective monarchy opens the field to factions."[3]

German liberalism, however, proved to be even more cautious, and it turned out to be very impure; extreme reactionary opinions were mixed with principles of progress.

There resulted a strange amalgam and astonishing confusions: nothing very seductive for profound spirits; nor anything which decisively surpassed Hegelian conceptions.

This vague liberalism inspired a few of the more important segments of the student movement after 1815. The patriots wanted to reform the style of student life, often rude and dissolute, to give it the seriousness requisite for service to the nation. They eliminated the former student associations, the old *Landmannschaften* where students had been grouped according to their home regions, and where there reigned a particularistic and aristocratic spirit (among them, for example, the associations of *Swabia, Saxonia, Borussia* and so on.)

They wanted to replace them with patriotic German associations. Their ideal was expressed in two catchwords: first *German unity*, then the *constitution*. This ideal inspired the new student associations, the *Burschenschaften*, that were born in each of the great German universities.

These associations still remained exclusive, limited to their university and to the state upon which it depended. Later, and particularly under the direct and decisive influence of Hegel's disciple, Carové, they united in a "general" *Burschenschaft*, welcoming all the students of Germany.

In this *Allgemeinen Burschenschaft* Carové and his friends battled, sometimes with success, against the remnants of xenophobia and anti-semitism inherited from the regional associations.

The most important tendency in this movement was nationalism, which had been aggravated by French occupation and oppression. This nationalism easily degenerated into manifestations of chauvinism and took the characteristic form called *Deutschtum*, something rather like *Germanization*. Enlightened minds, Hegel among them, condemned the excesses of this nationalism and so sometimes used the word *Deutschtum* in a pejorative sense.

The *Burschenschaft* did exhibit positive traits. But above all, it alone possessed them—and this is what gives it its relative importance. Such was the situation of the Germans, such was their economic, social, national and political misery that these student associations, in their total isolation from the rest of the nation, with their whims, their extravagance and their incoherence, represented German patriotism and German political life.

As well, absolutism and the feudal class, in the absence of any other declared enemies (if one sets aside the related opposition of the bureaucratic reformers) directed their main forces of repression against them.

In this national German distress, "Germanization" — despite its brutality, crudeness, and lack of political tact — accomplished a somewhat useful result. It contributed in a certain measure to reawakening a sense of the German nation. Engels noted this in his article on Arndt:

> On the other hand, one must not ignore the fact that Germanization (*Deutschtümelei*) was a necessary stage in the formation of our national spirit.[4]

2. Its Failings

In contrast to those features that were useful to the nation and politically beneficial, the *Burschenschaft* and *Deutschtum* displayed many tendencies that were unpleasant and disturbing.

At a time when he was still a bourgeois democrat and a very convinced liberal patriot, Engels thoroughly documented this negative side of the German nationalistic movement during the early years of the 19th century. Engels's criticisms are of direct interest here because they concur in many respects with those Hegel formulated.

In his article of June 1841 on Ernst Moritz Arndt, Engels explained the historical necessity of "Germanization". It derived from conditions inherent in the life of the German nation. Nonetheless it led to a "blind alley". Engels directed all his efforts to explaining why, after 1815, the patriotic Prussian movement became involved in this "blind alley of Germanization".[5]

The first characteristic of this passion for Germanization was *confusion*: "the positive elements with which it pleased itself lay buried in an obscurity from which they never quite emerged."[6]

Hegel came to the point of calling the "demagogues" "wretched" (he spoke of their *Jämmerlichkeit*[7]), while Engels labelled as paradoxical (*widersinnig*) a good many of their ideas.[8]

Hegel was first in his critique of *Deutschtum*, which, in a cruel pun, he called *Deutschdumm*: Germanic silliness.[9] More scholarly, and employing Hegelian vocabulary, Engels explained that,

> the Germanizing trend was negation, abstraction in the Hegelian sense. It created abstract Germans by stripping off everything that had not descended from national roots over sixty-four purely German generations.[10]

For his part, Karl Marx, in his *Contribution to the Critique of Hegel's Philosophy of Law* (1844), mocked the Germanizers who returned to "primeval Teutonic forests."[11]

Some members of the *Burschenschaft* themselves characterized Hegel's influence on their movement as serving to attenuate the excesses of Germanization. Thus Karl Förster wrote in his diary for 24 July 1820:

> Noon, a few friends at our place. Griesheim[12] speaks with great devotion of Hegel and of Hegel's influence in restraining exaggerated Germanization. He seems to present himself as a declared enemy of Fries.[13]

The role of Hegel's disciples in the *Burschenschaft*, in particular Carové, is enough to provide corroborative testimony.

The Germanizing members of the *Burschenschaft* felt a nostalgia for the middle ages and its social structure, which they pictured in idyllic terms. They affected the use of the ancient Germanic language, while purging it of all words of foreign derivation. Aping a medieval style, they decked themselves out in ridiculous costumes, wearing rapiers and all. And they took these childish practices very seriously.

Sensible minds were irritated by this attempt to pass off as the essence of German patriotism what was really a matter of youthful identity crises or student pranks. But at the same time they were well aware that serious regressive — and even feudal—tendencies inspired this preference for the middle ages, found as well in the romantic literature of the day, which conflicted with modern liberal aspirations.

With vigour Engels criticized this deplorable strand of German nationalism:

> Even its seemingly positive features were negative, for Germany could only be led towards its ideals by negating a whole century of her development, and thus its intention was to push the nation back into the Germanic Middle Ages or even into the primeval Germanic purity of the *Tuetoburger Wald*. Jahn embodied this trend in its extreme.[14]

Hegel took issue with this tendency, while making an effort to understand it. Without question he also opposed those who did not grasp its meaning and historical origin, and who therefore violently attacked it from a dogmatic point of view. On this point we have the testimony of Jahn himself. This picturesque leader of what one could call "folkloric nationalism" had been violently attacked by Steffens, whom he accused of having misrepresented his ideas on patriotic physical education in order the more easily to criticize them. In a letter of 1818 to an unknown correspondent Jahn wrote: "Hegel has also already taken a stand against these caricatures."[15]

The extravagant and unreflective nationalism of the members of the *Burschenschaft* frequently led them to the point of xenophobia. This was directed particularly against the recent invaders, the French. Engels pointed out the error of their way:

> It is against the French especially, whose invasion had been repulsed and whose hegemony in external matters is based on the fact that they master, more easily than all nations at least, the *form* of European culture, namely civilization—it is against the French that the iconoclastic fury was directed most of all.[16]

In the same manner, Paris always remained for Hegel "this capital of the civilized world";[17] he missed no opportunity to declare his attachment to France, to its thought and its history. This preference had its influence on certain decisions of his practical life: he registered his three sons in Berlin's French high school.[18]

From all that we know, Hegel could not have felt in the slightest any of the anti-French hatred that excited so many of the "demagogues". And all the less so in that there was grafted onto it a bitter hostility towards the French Revolution, its consequences and its memory.

On this point Engels described the conduct of the Germanizers:

> The great, eternal achievements of the revolution were abhorred as "foreign frivolities" or even "foreign lies and falsehoods"; no one thought of the kinship between this stupendous act of the people and the national uprising of 1813;* that which Napoleon had introduced, the emancipation of the Israelites, trial by jury, sound civil law in place of the pandects, was condemned solely because of its initiator. Hatred of the French became a duty.[19]

Hegel, as well, never renounced the teachings or the bourgeois achievements of the French Revolution, this "magnificent sunrise". In accordance with one progressive tradition in Germany, and like Engels later on, he viewed Napoleon as the successor and heir of the men of '89.[20]

Engels mentioned the intention of the Germanizers to revoke the emancipation of the Jews, brought to Germany at large by Napoleon, and introduced in Prussia by Hardenberg. We have come across Fries's antisemitism. Recall that the *Burschenschaft* occasionally participated in antisemitic pogroms, such as the one at Darmstadt.[21] In his *Philosophy of Right*, on the contrary, Hegel advocated granting civil rights to the Jews,[22] and in Berlin he associated with the most prominent among them.[23]

Finally, Hegel's realism certainly did not fail to take notice of the "demagogues'" isolation. There could have been little hope of an immediate political transformation based upon their movement, and one should refrain from attributing to them too great an importance. As Engels observed:

> Thus, the revolutionary party in Germany, from 1815 to 1839, consisted of *theorists* only. Its recruits were drawn from the universities; it was made up of none but students.[24]

To all of these negative features of the *Burschenschaft* let us add one more, certainly less important but irritating nonetheless. These nationalistic students all drew their swords at the drop of a hat. They were possessed by an incredible mania for duelling. The authorities could easily reproach them for this fault and to use it as a pretext for prosecution and imprisonment.

It is quite clear that an intelligent and informed German liberal could in no way approve of the *Burschenschaft*'s activities as a whole, even if overall his sympathies were pointed in that direction.

3. The Murder of Kotzebue

From 1819 on, German political life as a whole had to suffer the consequences of an event that took on significance only because the reaction used it as a pretext for intensifying its antidemocratic repression.

On 23 March 1819, the reactionary journalist, Kotzebue, a foe of "demagogues" and nationalists, and a spy for the Tsar in Germany, was assassinated in Mannheim by a member of the *Burschenschaft*, the student K.L. Sand.

Hinrichs, a disciple of Hegel, and one of the more "reactionary", announced the news to his master:

> You will perhaps have already heard that Kotzebue was stabbed to death on March 23rd at Mannheim by a Jena student. He came from Jena for the purpose. Kotzebue was stabbed four times after the student -- Sand, a native of the Erlangen area -- handed him a note stating "March 23rd is the day of Kotzebue's death." He then immediately went into the street in front of Kotzebue's house and inflicted two stab wounds on himself, wounds which are no doubt fatal, but which have not yet ended in death. On account of this event, this being the day of Kotzebue's funeral, the local [Heidelberg] student association is today in Mannheim.[25]

Notice the coolly objective tone of the account. Hinrichs does not seem greatly distressed by Kotzebue's demise. But then, he associated amicably with members of the *Burschenschaft* such as Hegel's friends, Henning and Förster.[26]

By chance, of Hegel's response to Hinrichs, which must without doubt have referred to this affair, there remains only a fragment, and that concerns other matters.[27]

Sand, the murderer of Kotzebue, was a theology student at the University of Jena and was known to be a friend of the leader of the *Burschenschaft*'s most determined faction, Karl Follen.[28] Recovered from his wounds and condemned to death, he was beheaded on May 5, 1820.

When he learned of Kotzebue's assassination, Metternich declared that, for his part, he had no doubt about how to make use of it. From then on the most stringent measures overwhelmed the *Burschenschaft*, the press, the nationalist liberal movement and the universities. Sand was not an *agent provocateur* but, unintentionally, he had played that role.

Apart from several fanatical members of the *Burschenschaft*, there were in the last analysis only a very few who approved Sand's action without reservation. But of those who condemned Sand in whole or in part, not all did so for the same reasons.

The feudal class, shocked by the progress of the "demagogues", which its own fear greatly exaggerated, and appalled by Sand's audacity, considered itself to be attacked in the person of Kotzebue. It condemned the assassin's ideology, his nationalism, and his hostility towards the government and the Holy Alliance. At the same time it praised Kotzebue's character, debatable though that was, and above all his political attitude.

From their side, the progressives assessed Sand's conduct in several ways. In general, they did not condemn his deepest motives: his patriotism and opposition to despotism. But some among them, taking a moral stand, rejected outright the use of crime as a means even when in the service of the best ends. Others, thinking in particular of the disastrous consequences which the event would bring in its train, emphasized how inadequate the means were for the end, and regretted the murderer's lack of political sense.

At times these two points of view converged. Hegel seems to have disapproved of the assassination of individuals. Without doubt he had been given quite detailed information about Sand, a disturbed and tormented spirit, who believed himself entrusted with a sort of divine mission and, like an omniscient judge, had decided on his own what had to be done.

Sand's personality and behaviour greatly resembled those of the fanatic individualists Hegel had always detested. One could easily apply to him the criticism which, in the *Aesthetics*, was directed at the hero of Schiller's *Robbers*, Karl Moor. Hegel wrote:

> Universal ends, like those pursued by Karl Moor and Wallenstein, cannot be accomplished by a single individual by making others his obedient instruments; on the contrary, such ends prevail by their own force, sometimes with the will of the many, sometimes against it and without their knowledge.[29] *

Contempt for, and aversion to, Kotzebue did not necessarily imply approval of Sand. In his study on Solger, Hegel quoted Solger's opinion of Sand:

> But now the *foolish stupidity*, to want to save the fatherland by means of the murder of the old milksop! The *cold, insolent pride*, to condemn the so-called evil in the manner of a *minor judge of the world*! The *empty hypocrisy* with oneself with respect to religion....[30]

Doubtless Hegel was not as irritated with Sand as Solger was: the remarks of his disciple Carove on Kotzebue's murder are enough to suggest this. Hegel seems to have reproached Sand primarily for having used crime, in a purely individual decision and in a rash manner.

Such reproaches do not present us with a reactionary character. Mehring did not assess Sand's action very differently:

> Rooted in lofty motives, the deed itself was politically senseless; however, it was all the more welcomed by the despotic, feudal reaction, which had been lying in wait for a long time.[31]

Disapproval of Kotzebue's murder was widespread, and deserved.

4. De Wette

A colleague of Hegel was an exception, however, believing it to be his duty to take up Sand's defence. Professor de Wette sent a letter to the assassin's mother. To be sure, he did not express approval of Sand's action, attributing it to error and passion. Nevertheless, while condemning the act, he largely absolved the actor.

Sand had acted in the conviction that he was perfectly right and he was a pure and pious young man: for de Wette this was what mattered. In his eyes, it was good for each person always to follow his conscience and, on this basis, Sand's action would continue to provide a beautiful testimonial of his time.

De Wette attempted to justify an objectively reprehensible act by the attitude of mind in which it had been performed. In fact he showed sympathy for a guilty person, which implied condemnation of the government.

As soon as de Wette's letter became known it aroused numerous protests, among Kotzebue's opponents as much as his friends. The former would not accept the sort of justification de Wette provided; or they considered this letter to be as ill-judged as the assassination itself.

The king had earlier promulgated a cabinet decree which withdrew the right to teach from any individual guilty of spreading ideas dangerous to the state. A rapidly convened inquiry commission suspended de Wette from his functions without notice.

Appeals made by de Wette, as well as an attempt at intervention by the senate of the university, were curtly rejected by the king.

De Wette then tendered a letter of resignation: convinced of his innocence, he had decided to withdraw from his majesty's territories. Students came in a delegation to give him a silver cup, engraved with a verse from Saint Matthew, and de Wette left for Weimar proudly refusing a term's salary, offered "out of good will".

De Wette's colleagues were almost unanimous in regretting the sending of his famous letter, but they were no more in favour of the king's attitude or that of his government; this manner of treating de Wette placed in question freedom of opinion as well as academic freedom.

Some, Schleiermacher among them, denied that the government possessed the right to dismiss a professor. Others, Hegel among them (at least according to Schleiermacher), "agreed that the state could suspend a professor upon the condition that it continued to pay his salary." This small difference in interpretation widened the breach between Schleiermacher and Hegel.[32]

Nevertheless, everyone condemned the government's measure. Each could from then on dread denunciation; no one continued to feel secure in his employment.

De Wette had a wife and children. He had lost all hope of finding a professional position in a member country of the Holy Alliance. Taking into account the place, the date and the circumstances, his colleagues adopted a quite remarkable approach to his situation. They secretly organized a collection with the purpose of assuring the victim a year's salary. According to the testimony of Link, reported by Varnhagen, the government never knew anything of this clandestine show of solidarity — fortunately for the donors,[33] among whom could be found not only Hegel but also Savigny himself!

A philosophical opponent of Hegel, de Wette was a former student and a faithful friend of Fries. The way he explained and excused Sand's conduct went completely against Hegel's views on the moral insufficiency of subjective conviction.

Nevertheless, Hegel contributed 25 thalers for de Wette, a large enough sum, since it represented about four days of salary, and his resources continued to be modest. This contribution expressed neither personal sympathy (de Wette had tried everything to prevent Hegel's nomination to Berlin; he had supported Fries's candidacy!), philosophical kinship, nor moral approval: it signified political solidarity, the support accorded to a man subject to arbitrary government sanction.

5. Hegel and the Burschenschaft

In reality, despite the serious faults and internal contradictions of the *Burschenschaft*, Hegel could not but feel close to it.

We need to notice that the movement started at the universities of Giessen and Jena. Since Hegel had lived in the latter city for a good while, he knew the key advocates of the association. Jena students had organized the festival of the *Wartburg*. With the exception of Fries, the professors who took part in the ceremony were Hegel's old friends: the naturalist Oken, also a victim of political repression, with whom Hegel never ceased to correspond on friendly terms; Kieser, the medical doctor, to whom he sent his "best wishes" even after *Wartburg*;[34] and Schweitzer.

All these friends of the *Burschenschaft* frequently visited the home of Frommann the bookseller, Hegel's close friend: in this family Hegel's illegitimate son, the little Ludwig Fischer, had been raised, and at this home Hegel took refuge during the battle of Jena. Frommann, who had demonstrated considerable generosity to Hegel, and a great deal of confidence in him, was sympathetic to the leaders of the *Burschenschaft*; he welcomed to his home the historian Luden—famous for his polemic against Kotzebue— whose attacks against this disparaged writer perhaps incited the assassination attempt of 1819.

Hegel could not have condemned outright an association which included so many of his friends, colleagues and students.

But in addition he was virtually tied to it through family connections. Mrs. Frommann's sister, Betty Wesselhöft, whose name frequently occurs in Hegel's correspondence, provided an almost maternal care to the little Ludwig Fischer, who boarded with her for some time. The Wesselhöfts served as an adoptive family for Hegel's illegitimate son, and as a second home for the philosopher. Their name figures often in Fischer's album.

Hegel was therefore very well acquainted with Frommann's two nephews, two young physicians, Doctors Robert and William Wesselhöft, about whom he spoke as friends of his son.[35]

In the name of the Jena *Burschenschaft* Robert Wesselhöft had, in 1817, sent out announcements for the *Wartburg* festival to mark the fourth anniversary of the Battle of Leipzig and the three-hundredth anniversary of the Reformation.

The two Wesselhöft brothers devoted all their energies to developing the German democratic and national movement. Robert in particular, a member of the secret leadership, made a decisive contribution towards radicalizing and "politicizing" the *Burschenschaft*.[36]

Pursued by the police, Robert and William soon had to seek exile in Switzerland, where they found a great number of refugees, among them Snell, Follen, and Arnold Ruge.[37]

Frommann's son had also taken part in the *Wartburg* festival, of which he published an account.[38] Practically all the sons of Hegel's friends were adherents of the *Burschenschaft*: Gustav Asverus, the son of his Jena lawyer; Julius Niethammer; and so on. The patriotic student association recruited even from his wife's family: Mrs. Hegel's younger brother, Gottlieb von Tucher, who lived in Berlin with Hegel, was a close friend of Gustav Asverus and Julius Niethammer, participated actively in debates of the *Burschenschaft*,[39] and wrote some revolutionary letters which the police confiscated at his friends' homes.[40] In one of them he exclaimed: "When ever will the blood-red morning dawn?"

The patriotic movement included almost all students. As a result nearly all of Hegel's "auditors", students and disciples belonged to the *Burschenschaft* for a longer or shorter time, and were more or less actively militant. Some among them played a role of the first rank in the political fights, the incidents involving police and the ideological conflicts of the epoch.

Without doubt, Hegel received direct and detailed information about what was happening in the *Burschenschaft* and in the nationalist and constitutional movement. His informers could be found at the family table and in the offices and classrooms of the university; he ran into them on walks and around card tables.

Hegel kept a watch on the "demagogues", on occasion passing a severe but justified judgement on their escapades. But he also tried to guide them by offering advice and by discussing the principles of their action with them. He often mingled with them, in their festivities and their debates.

But the area where Hegel's devotion to the "demagogues" appears most vividly, because irrefutable documents remain, is to be found in his defence of the persecuted against the actions of the police and the courts. On this matter, judicial archives preserve evidence of much of Hegel's activity, even though, understandably, he himself observed great discretion concerning his relations with the political opposition.

Hegel once called a friend of his an "advocate of the oppressed" (*Sachwalter der Bedrängten*).[41] But this friend, Krause, was performing his professional duties, whereas, without any professional obligation, with complete altruism and not without running great risks, Hegel performed a long and varied series of acts that much more strongly qualify him for the same title.

NOTES

1. F. Ponteil, *L'éveil des nationalités (1815-1848)* (Paris, 1960) 55. (Do not confuse this work with one bearing the same title by G. Weill, cited above, p. 48. n.16.)

2. Ibid. 55.

3. Ibid. 57.

4. Engels, "Ernst Moritz Arndt" in Marx-Engels, *Collected Works* (New York, 1975) II, 141.

5. Ibid. 140.

6. Ibid.

7. *Briefe* II, 271; *Letters,* 470.

8. Engels, 140.

9. *Briefe* II, 43; *Letters,* 312.

10. Engels, 140.

11. K. Marx, "Contribution to the Critique of Hegel's Philosophy of Law. Introduction" in Marx-Engels, *Collected Works*, III, 177.

12. To this member of the *Burschenschaft*, a student of Hegel, we owe the best transcripts of the philosopher's lectures at the University of Berlin.

13. Cited by Hoffmeister, *Briefe*, II, 482.

14. Engels, 140-141.

15. Cited by Hoffmeister, *Briefe,* III, 369.

16. Engels, 141.

17. *Briefe* III, 183; *Letters,* 649.

18. See *Briefe* IV, 127.

19. Engels, 141.

20. Hegel's praise of Napoleon can be compared with the Napoleonic poems of the young Engels ("The Emperor's Procession", and "St. Helena" [Marx-Engels, *Collected Works* II, 153-4, 131]) and with those of Heine ("The Grenadiers", etc.).

21. *Briefe* II 447-8 (notes of Hoffmeister).

22. *Philosophy of Right,* #270, note.

23. See Karl Hegel, *Leben und Erinnerungen* (Leipzig, 1910), 13.

24. "The Situation in Germany," in Marx-Engels, *Collected Works*, VI, 30.

25. *Briefe,* II, 215; *Letters,* 445.

26. See *Briefe,* III, 21.

27. *Briefe* II 215; *Letters,* 478.

28. An account of these events may be found in Schnabel, *Deutsche Geschichte im Neunzehnten Jahrhundert* (Freiburg, 1949) II, 254.

29. Hegel, *Aesthetics, Lectures on Fine Art*, tr. Knox, (Oxford, 1975) II, 1224.

30. Hegel, *Berliner Schriften*, (Hamburg, 1956), 171.

31. F. Mehring, *op.cit.* 228.

32. See *Briefe* II, 450. Note of Hoffmeister.

33. On all this one may consult Hoffmeister's remarks, *Briefe,* II, 445-47.

34. *Briefe* II, 204; *Letters,* 436.

35. *Briefe* II, 204; *Letters,* 436. See *Hegel secret*, 1st part, Chapter 2.

36. See K. Obermann, *Deutschland, 1815-1849* (Berlin, 1961) 44.

37. See, Oechsli, *op.cit.* 696.

38. See above, page 91, n.15.

39. See *Briefe* II, 433, note of Hoffmeister.

40. Ibid. 437.

41. With reference to his friend, the lawyer Krause, in a "private" letter to Niethammer. *Briefe* II, 323.

III

"The Advocate of the Oppressed"

A thousand powerful and subtle links tied Hegel to the bourgeois and progressive ideology of his time. This ideology was personified in a few leaders of the Burschenschaft and some isolated liberals.

These men suffered the persecution meted out by a somewhat reactionary government which mobilized its police and courts against them. The repression assumed a breadth that bore no relationship to the real danger that its opponents posed to established institutions.

The sanctions affected students and professors above all: dismissal, suspension, fines, imprisonment, exclusion from the university, residence under surveillance, detention in the citadel, and so on. The judges often showed extreme severity. For example, Arnold Ruge, the future founder of the *Hallischen Jahrbücher*, in which Marx would collaborate, was as a member of the *Burschenschaft* condemned in 1826 to fourteen years imprisonment in a fortress. He fortunately benefited from an early release and remained in prison for only a few years—just long enough to become acquainted with Hegelian philosophy, which then as well as later he in no way considered to be conservative.

Other "demagogues" would elude the sanctions only by becoming expatriots. Many of them settled in Switzerland and America.

The denunciations and arrests multiplied. In this atmosphere of terror most professors, particularly those in Berlin, adopted a prudent attitude and avoided getting involved or compromising themselves.

In contrast, Hegel took an active part in a very great number of celebrated judicial cases, courageously undertaking to defend the "demagogues" who found themselves prosecuted, and trying as much as was in his power to snatch them from their unhappy fate.

1. The Sources

Sometimes in his letters Hegel mentions these events and his own participation. The very nature of his correspondents suggests his preoccupations and efforts. Nevertheless, for readily understandable reasons, Hegel's *Letters* remain silent about most of the facts, and when they are referred to it is almost always only by allusion.*

Our principal source of information is the archives of the Prussian Ministry of the Interior. They conserve what it was in the interest of the police and the courts to know and keep on record. Hegel would undoubtedly have preferred to see these reports disappear in his own day; on his own, he would not have allowed them to remain. They contained evidence of his friendly relations with the "demagogues" and of his interventions on their behalf: compromising documents indeed!

In the notes which embellish his edition of Hegel's *Letters*, J. Hoffmeister has published some of these documents. For this we must be grateful. Here is a most significant contribution to a better knowledge of the man, Hegel. Hoffmeister has finally made it possible for us to refer to texts that had remained inaccessible until now. Nevertheless, before citing and commenting upon them, we need to add a few remarks.

First of all it must be emphasized that this publication of documents in the notes of an edition of the *Letters* remains of necessity very incomplete; and its editor in no way tries to hide this fact. What is the relative importance of what has thus come to our attention? The example of the Cousin affair offers us a way of answering this question.

Victor Cousin's arrest in Germany, its judicial and diplomatic consequences, as well as Hegel's intervention, take up *four pages* of Hoffmeister's notes.[1] But the editor himself mentions that in the single Prussian national archives from which he drew them, *four thick volumes* of documents are devoted to Cousin. One page of notes per volume of documents!

In addition, Hoffmeister could not consult the French archives or Cousin's papers; it is clear he did not even refer to studies published in France on the subject.

This example serves to show the relative scarcity of published documents. We can only regret this.

The inquests, the proceedings and the disputes concerning Cousin certainly stretched on and on: a good business for court clerks drafting interminable transcripts, reports and memoranda.

But other trials in which Hegel was involved assumed almost as much importance in the eyes of the authorities: thus the case of Carové and that of Förster, both taking a long time to be settled, came before diverse tribunals, involved a number of people and intersected with other similar cases.

In the jumble of documents available to him, and quite apart from those which remained inaccessible or unknown, Hoffmeister was therefore obliged to select: highlighting certain texts, ignoring others, editing and summarizing.

As far as we can tell, he did it honestly, and as objectively as possible. But even if we do then accord him our confidence, we still have to ask about the frame of reference for his approach.

In an enquiry of this sort, the choice and the evaluation of events and testimonies depend greatly on the view one has of the state, the police and the courts, and on the approach to them that might or could be taken by civil servants generally, and those of the university in particular.

In our opinion Hoffmeister's notes betray the imprecision and obscurity of his political ideas. As a result it is very difficult to assess what he means by "extremism" in the *Burschenschaft*, or by the "innocence" of an accused "demagogue". Having examined the documents used to develop his arguments, we are tempted not to agree with most of his conclusions.

Another difficulty: the valuable documentation, of which a few fragments are provided by Hoffmeister, consists essentially of informer and police reports, of depositions by detainees and witnesses, of letters written by prisoners, and of petitions addressed by those in unfortunate circumstances to those reponsible for their detention.

All of these will reveal their real meaning only when account is taken of their particular circumstances. Hoffmeister seems to have taken such texts too literally. Those who spoke or wrote knew that their fate hung upon this expression of their thought; without question, then, they frequently held back from expressing themselves too openly.

One may well doubt the sincerity of a declaration of submission made by a detainee after six weeks' imprisonment. One may question the reality, importance and comprehensiveness of the personal associations which a suspect admits to the police when he is first being interrogated. One has the right to "interpret" the deferential expressions used by a petitioner in a letter to an important and formidable person.

It is clear that Hoffmeister failed to follow through in this way.

Let us add a third difficulty: all or almost all we know of Hegel's associations with the "demagogues" is provided by the official archives. The Prussian police deployed an intense and co-ordinated campaign that was not inefficient. As well, the inexperience and naiveté of the "demagogues" helped the police in their task. Nevertheless, do we have to believe that everyone was caught, that none of their activity escaped from the informers, the investigators and the rozzers?

Without doubt some able adversaries of the government outwitted the investigations and inquiries. Quite likely Hegel was connected with a few "demagogues" who did not fall into the snares of the police. But it was in his interest not to leave any vestige of these liaisons. The smallest trace that we could discover would then be worth more than twenty kilos of police archives concerning a member of the opposition who was arrested, interrogated and judged.

All of this calls into question the value of certain judgements made by Hoffmeister. How can we but smile when we see him conclude, after examining each affair, that the suspect whose cause Hegel had taken up was "innocent"?

Innocent Carové, Asverus and Ulrich, Förster and Victor Cousin!

But according to this account absolutely all of the nationalists and constitutionalists apprehended by the police were innocent. They could not be accused of any particular crime ...except that which was the most serious in the eyes of the reactionaries: just to be nationalistic partisans of a constitution, opponents of the Prussian King's policies and those of the Mainz Commission, enemies of Metternich and the Holy Alliance!

Hoffmeister seems to believe that in these cases the police and administration operated in a way that was neutral: that they prosecuted only real crimes, as seen from the perspective of eternal justice.

But from that perspective, it is the King of Prussia and his henchmen whom they ought to have accused. Betrayal of national interests, arbitrary violence, contempt for the law and the rights of the people are found on this side. Perjury was also to be found here, for most of the members of the opposition called for no more than what Frederick William III had refused to carry out, despite having made solemn promises.

The patriots and volunteers of 1813 became impatient.G. Weill explains their discontent in this way:

> They had been promised constitutions, because the 1813 movement was as much liberal as nationalist. The Grand Duke of Saxony-Weimar, the friend of Goethe, was the first to keep his word. But all the liberals of Germany awaited with impatience Prussia's decision. Chancellor Hardenberg had in fact been thinking for many years of a representative system; at the Vienna Congress, he had proposed that Frederick William grant it upon the day of his solemn return to Berlin. He applied even more pressure after Napoleon's return from Elba, and obtained an edict from the king, dated May 22, 1815, in which Frederick William finally promised "to the Prussian nation" to give it a constitution "by means of a written act". Made public a few days after Waterloo, the edict of 1815 aroused great hopes—but the months passed and the constitution did not appear. A muted but obstinate struggle continued in the entourage of Frederick William between the chancellor, always influential, and the absolutist faction, who distrusted this "Jacobin" ... Postponing the constitution, the monarch limited himself in the interim to creating a council of state.[2]

Hoffmeister, therefore, was right to regard the German democrats as "innocent". Even better, when they timidly took action, they became authentic dispensers of justice. The real "conspiracies against the nation" and "secret intrigues" were hatched in the royal court, where "coalitions" of interests were operating, where "liaisons against legitimate authority" — that of Hardenberg — were knit together. Before the judgement of history (*Weltgeschichte, Weltgericht*)[3], the Prussian reactionaries are seated in the dock of the accused, whereas all the exiles, the imprisoned and the dispossessed remind them of their crimes.

The patriots and progressive Prussians have on their side "the noble law of history", as Hegel himself would have said. Nevertheless it is obvious that neither the police nor the courts of Frederick William acted according to this law. Those whom it exonerated, Frederick William covered with disgrace. Those whom it cleared of guilt were, for the men of the restoration, the incarnation of crime par excellence: the spirit of progress.

So Hegel always intervened in favour of innocents, to be sure. But no less certainly, in the eyes of the Prussian reaction, these innocents represented the worst of the guilty. It is not "by mistake" or by "being overzealous" or by excess of stupidity that the police rounded them up, as Hoffmeister so often suggests. On the contrary, the published documents show that, except in a few cases, the police did not arrest just anyone at random.

They seized quite precisely those whom they sought and those whom they had the explicit mission to "neutralize": the opponents of absolutism and the Holy Alliance, the partisans of national unity and the constitution.

Without knowing it, Hoffmeister restricted the scope of Hegel's interventions by always insisting upon the "innocence" of his protegés. Thus he implies that one has nothing to fear when one defends the innocent!

In reality, Hegel exposed himself to the hatred and vengeance of the reactionaries much more than Hoffmeister, in making his half-hearted attempt to rehabilitate the "state philosopher", realized. How could the really guilty parties, the king and his court, the feudal class and their police servants, pardon Hegel for impeding at every moment their repressive projects? How could the investigators and judges not have realized that Hegel placed himself every time in the same relative position: not on their side but against them.

2. Pretexts and Reasons for the Persecutions

When one first opens the record of Hegel's interventions in favour of the "demagogues", what is striking is their number, as well as the importance, duration and complexity of the cases involved. One notices as well that they are spread over a long period of Hegel's residence at Berlin.

When the various other incidents provoked by Hegel's teaching are added, it can be seen that, in Berlin, Hegel had really seen, as he put it, "a storm rise up every year";[4] however, the atmosphere became particularly oppressive at certain times such as 1819.

We offer below an approximate calendar of the principal events that were for Hegel the cause of anxiety, personal difficulty or interventions in favour of others.

Date and Nature of the Events

August 11, 1818	Förster bound over to a military tribunal.
March 3, 1819	Assassination attempt by Sand.
April 8, 1819	Asverus arrested.
May 2, 1819	Hegel goes to the festival of Pichelsburg.
July 8, 1819	Von Henning arrested.
July 14, 1819	Ulrich arrested.
November, 1819	Beginning of Carové's investigation.
End of 1819	De Wette's letter and collection for him.
1820	Carlsbad congress
June, 1821	Royal decree against teaching Oken's "atheistic" philosophy.
Beginning of 1823	Ulrich reinstated, then later, Förster.
October 15, 1824	Victor Cousin arrested.
December 8, 1824	Asverus condemned to six years in prison.
November 20, 1825	The Cousin case settled.
1826	Birthday celebration of Hegel and Goethe.
July 17, 1826	The Asverus case settled.
1827	Catholic complaint against Hegel. Suspicions following his trip to Paris and an article in the *Constitutionnel*.

1829	Schubärt accuses Hegel of atheism and hostility to the state.
1831	Warning from the crown prince about Gans.
	Censorship of the second part of Hegel's article on the *Reform Bill*.

The most "thorny" cases involved Asverus, Ulrich, Carové, Förster and Cousin.

The pretext for each arrest or prosecution varied. But the real motive remained fundamentally the same. Let us examine a few examples that will let us discern both the common characteristics of these cases of repression and their more significant differences. At the same time we will discover variations in the differential between the official charge and the ends really aimed at by the authorities.

Henning

First of all, the arrest which on the surface appears the most unjust and even the most absurd is probably that of Henning. It was initiated on the basis of quotations taken from letters, not written by him, but addressed to him. A letter from his mother-in-law seemed to have particularly caught the attention of the police![5]

Upon closer examination, however, one discovers that the police did not strike at Henning by chance. Would they have watched his mail had he not seemed suspect? In following his trail, they were not on the wrong track. And in arresting him, upon whatever pretext, they surely hit upon a member of the opposition guilty of the critical offence which they refrained from explicitly mentioning: the offence of having an opinion.

The police knew that it is not far from opinion to action. Henning thought, but he spoke as well, spread his ideas, linked himself with suspect individuals and even to some already judged and condemned. 'A friend of Friedrich Förster[6], of Carové and of Asverus; he probably belongs to the *Burschenschaft*.'

When von Wittgenstein, one of the leaders of the feudal party, denounced Carové to Altenstein, he pointed out as an aggravating circumstance Carové's connections with Henning and Asverus. In the course of the Carové trial, Henning was confronted with Asverus, who himself acknowledged the existence of their association.[7]

We do not know exactly what Henning's opinions were during this period. We only know that at the time he came forward as the propagandist for Napoleonic ideas—the "Corsican monster" was then the object of the Prussian reactionaries' hatred and the distribution of his writing was strictly prohibited. Varnhagen reports this fact in a letter of 1822, some time after Henning's trial:

> Doctor von Henning has recently delivered an impassioned apology of Napoleon, of his life and government: he praised him to the skies.[8]

This Napoleonic—and subversive—tendency of Henning was shared by Hegel. The latter fervently sought out documents on Napoleon, and Henning forwarded some to him,[9] while van Ghert sent from Holland works prohibited in Prussia.

After his release, Henning went to Saxe-Weimar—the "stronghold of Jacobinism", according to the men of the Holy Alliance—and upon the recommendation of Hegel he established contact with Goethe.

Detained for six weeks, Henning was watched night and day by a guard in his cell: his case was not considered insignificant. Hegel's teaching assistant was treated with the utmost suspicion and in a most undignified manner. Hegel was certainly in no way unaware of the political attitude of his student.

Asverus

The pretexts for prosecutions against the "demagogues" were sometimes made more precise even though they still remained divorced from their deeper causes. Thus the first arrest of Asverus happened in Berlin upon the request of Jena University, where he had earlier studied. He was accused of duelling, a common enough infraction in the student life of the epoch, no great matter.

But Asverus belonged to the *Burschenschaft* and vehemently maintained antigovernment opinions. The police became aware of these in letters to his friends, which they seized. They had caught an adversary and would not soon let him go.

Asverus's imprudent declarations in some of the letters opened by the secret police allowed them to accuse him of making "death threats" against a former "collaborator" with the French at Jena. Asverus tried to justify himself; his declarations seem to us singularly embarrassed.[10]

In so far as we can judge so long after the events using the documents available, Asverus does not have a clear conscience. It is only by ignoring the main point of the affair and by sticking to legal formalities that Hoffmeister could denounce

> not only the injustice of the judgement but also the questionable pretexts under which Asverus was held for so long in detention.[11]

The police and judges simply did not possess formal proof of Asverus's guilt. His trial nonetheless lasted seven years with numerous periods of detention and all sorts of incidents, until, in 1826, the king in an act of clemency ordered an end to the affair. From the point of view of judicial form, the attitude of Frederick William's police and judicial system arouses indignation. They chose their pretexts unadvisedly, did not succeed in obtaining the necessary witnesses, and so proceeded arbitrarily with regard to the accused.

And yet at the bottom of it all we cannot believe that there is "judicial error" here. Asverus represented the type of man whose voice the feudal class was interested in stifling, and whose political activity they were interested in cutting short. He clearly belonged to the category of those needing to be "check-mated".

In being particularly active in Asverus's defence, then, Hegel was not seeking to save a young man *wrongly* accused of patriotism and liberalism. On the contrary, he tried to protect a patriot, whom the authorities were *in the wrong* in persecuting.

Hegel, a realist and well aware of the *Burschenschaft's* affairs, could not have been unmindful of what was hidden behind the alleged pretexts. He knew well enough what were the real purposes: to repress constitutional tendencies, to disperse nationalist factions, and to intimidate and eliminate the militants.

Ulrich

In the case of Karl Ulrich, duelling again served as a pretext. This hot-head, who got into a fight at the drop of a hat, was nicknamed "Furioso".

But this propensity for duelling was grafted onto a well-known ideological bent. The fanatical duellists were recruited among the members of the opposition, among the proponents of "patriotic gymnastics". Ulrich was accused as well of leading a cheer in honour of Jahn.

In fact the cause of the persecution against Ulrich appeared clearly during his trial. His political attitude was that of an obstinate member of the opposition, almost of a rebel. In 1818 he had actively participated in establishing the Berlin *Burschenschaft*, and he became its president in 1819. His personal associations were tied to "demagogic" circles. He was accused of professing "political principles entirely corrupt and absolutely incompatible with service to the state."[12]

Arrested on July 14, 1819, he was first held in preventive custody for one hundred and ten days. He was released, but then his trial began and harsh administrative measures interrupted the course of his studies. He was arrested again in February 1820, whereupon the senate of the University protested. He was then subjected to a variety of vexing administrative moves; harrassment did not cease until the beginning of 1823.

Ulrich did not have political ideas that were very clear, but he compensated for his ideological uncertainties with considerable obstinacy in practice. For the entire duration of his case, he kept a particularly courageous attitude, refusing to concede and maintaining his pluck for a long time in spite of the blows directed against him.

In associating himself closely with Ulrich, Hegel knew what he was doing: he took sides, and certainly not those of the police and administration. He was not unaware of the dangers he thereby faced.

Carové

With regard to Carové the pretext for the prosecution approached its true purpose. In 1819 Hegel's teaching assistant published a pamphlet: *Concerning the Assassination of Kotzebue*. Its author did not agree with Sand's act, but he explained it in a politico-philosophical way that hardly coincided with the official condemnations and even at times contradicted them.

The police had known of Carové for a long time because of his leading role in the *Burschenschaft*. As a founding member he had made a long speech at the *Wartburg* festival, and his intervention often proved decisive in the internal debates to set the ideological approach of the organization.

In general he is to be considered a moderate, opposed to the extremists within the *Burschenschaft*. But *moderate* does not here mean *less progressive*. On the contrary! Carové's "moderation" consisted in arguing against the excessive teutomaniacs and for the admission of foreigners and Jews to the *Burschenschaft*.

Carové's publication about the Sand affair provoked somewhat of a scandal in reactionary circles. When Carové then applied for the position of official teaching assistant in Hegel's course at the University of Berlin, the Prince von Wittgenstein took on himself the trouble of denouncing him to Altenstein:

> As you know, Mr. Carové has published under his own name a pamphlet for the praise and defence of the assassination committed by Sand, of which I have recently read a review that was quite prejudicial to the author. This Mr. Carové was to be found in Breslau in good company, and his company here—Henning, Förster and Schulze[13]—are well chosen too! By this one also sees what kind of associations the latter has with Henning. Taking into account the opinions which he has expressed publicly, Mr. Carové does not seem to be at all a man whom we should permit to teach.[14]

No less could Hegel have been unaware of Carové's real opinions and therefore of the true motive for the prosecution, since the latter, in his pamphlet on Sand, seems to have been directly inspired by his master's ideas. He himself expressly derives his position on Sand from Hegelian principles; even Hoffmeister allows that in this work "Sand's action is judged from Hegel's point of view."[15]

Wittgenstein's attacks sharpened and were renewed. The prince even had a long refutation of Carové's theses written by a certain Pauli. He put into motion the full judicial machinery.

From all indications, it was Hegel who, by way of Carové, was already at this time the focus of interest. Hoffmeister notes: "In this whole affair, the court cabal, in the person of Wittgenstein, turned its attention for the first time against Hegel."

He also adds that "in this attack Carové was an innocent victim, in that, through his writing and its sensitive topic, he offered an easy target."[16]

Hoffmeister exaggerates: we must doubt the "innocence" of Carové, who was a member of the political opposition that controlled the *Burschenschaft*, and who continued to be "ahead of his time" to the end of his life.

It is indeed not impossible that Hegel urged him to write this essay on Sand, which Carové even drew to Altenstein's attention at the very time he was renewing his request for appointment. In any event Hegel did not discourage this initiative of his disciple, who would certainly have consulted him about it.

The court probably reacted more violently than the two philosophers had expected. It took aim at a philosophy that did not suit it and that it knew many demagogues were adopting.

Note well the date of this first assault against Hegel by the reaction in Berlin: 1819, scarcely one year after his arrival.

It was not at the end of Hegel's life that the "restorers" turned against him, as is often claimed. From the beginning they had discerned him to be their adversary.

Förster

Frederick Förster was prosecuted precisely for what he had done quite overtly. To a more clear-cut action there corresponded a more immediate repression.

He was not unknown to the public when the law began to be interested in him. Heroic fighter in the wars of liberation and wounded several times in battle, he had been the companion of the poet Theodore Körner, author of so many celebrated patriotic songs, who had been killed in combat. Förster also had served in the volunteer light infantry corps of Lützow, who as leaders of the popular uprising were particularly dear to Prussian patriots; and on the field of battle he had recorded the last words of the national heroine, Elinor Prochaska, discovering at the moment she died the deception thanks to which this young girl had been able to take part in the war.

Förster composed patriotic poems in which were relived the great events and moving incidents of the Prussian national awakening, of the original guerilla conflict, and then of the full-fledged, conventional war.

He represented the typical young Prussian intellectual, animated by a dual ideal: German unity and the liberalization of political life. When the post-war period did not fulfil the promise of the patriotic enthusiasm of 1813, Förster was profoundly disappointed.

And he did not hide it. In 1818 he published an article in which he directly attacked the chief of police, von Kamptz, and this in a journal published by Luden in Weimar that was detested by the reactionaries: *Nemesis*. In it Förster bemoaned the absence of a Prussian constitution and attacked the government and civil servants, accusing them of creating a gulf of misunderstanding between the king and his subjects. He vigorously took to task in particular the royal court, which he denounced for its intrigues and scheming against the king and people.[17]

Von Kamptz was easily able to exonerate himself from the precise accusations that Förster had made against him somewhat too superficially, without being certain of the facts.

Because of the article in *Nemesis* Förster was suspended and deprived of the chair he then occupied at the military school.

A public debate ensued and several articles protested against this dismissal, particularly in the newspapers of Saxe-Weimar. This engendered fresh diplomatic friction between that country and Prussia.

Accused of the crimes of high treason and libel against top officials, Förster was court-marshalled. But the supreme military tribunal took some cognizance of his conduct and acquitted him. In the army as well certain patriotic and liberal tendencies were retained.

The court and the ministry did not consider themselves defeated and despite his acquittal Förster was excluded from teaching and administration until 1823, the date when he obtained a new, non-teaching post, probably due to Hegel's intervention.

In Förster's case there can be no doubt: the man made no secret of his opposition to the regime; he proclaimed it. This was not an "unjust" or "absurd" assault by the reactionaries against an insignificant or inactive person, but rather a struggle between parties. In this struggle, Hegel sided with Förster.

Victor Cousin

The Cousin affair deserves longer treatment. It pits a French philosopher against a Prussian police working closely with the French police. It gives us access to the particular methods used by the adversaries with whom Hegel had to deal: their tortuous procedures, their tricks and their rivalries.

By examining it we can in retrospect throw light on the behaviour of the "demagogues" and reveal their serious shortcomings and the frailty of their endeavours at the same time as we unveil the baseness of their enemies. The threads of several similar intrigues intersect here, and we can see the names of the most important reactionaries mentioned next to those of the most notorious "conspirators". The case developed along ideological, as well as investigative, judicial, diplomatic and political lines. Into what a hornet's nest Hegel risked falling when he interceded for Victor Cousin! But his intervention no doubt contributed ultimately to thwarting the initiative of a despicable police force.

On October 15, 1824, at the request of the Mainz Commission, the government of Saxony proceded to arrest Victor Cousin in Dresden. The news caused a world-wide sensation. People wondered what motive had pressed the Saxon police into taking such spectacular action. We now know that they were the instruments of distant machinations, and that Cousin's arrest resulted from a whole series of measures secretly taken against him.

Deprived in 1820 of all official posts after his courses at the Sorbonne had been suspended, Victor Cousin had become for a while tutor for the sons of the Duchess of Montebello, widow of Field Marshal Lannes. In 1824, one of them decided to marry a young woman from Dresden. The Duchess of Montebello, not being able to travel, charged Cousin with the task of accompanying her son to Dresden and establishing contact with the family of her future daughter-in-law.

At first sight, then, Cousin's voyage to Dresden presented a harmless appearance. It nevertheless raised the suspicions of the French police—at least they thought they could take advantage of it. It is they who launched the "Cousin Affair."

At the moment when Cousin, without suspecting what was brewing, left for Germany, the director of the French police had a confidential note delivered to the Prussian minister plenipotentiary in France which ran thus:

MINISTRY OF THE INTERIOR
Department of Police

Paris, September 10, 1824

Confidential

To the Prussian Minister Plenipotentiary in Paris,

Baron, Sir,

I have the honour to inform you that the Duke of Montebello has just obtained a passport in order to go to Dresden where he says he is to be married. He is accompanied by a Mr. Cousin, professor of philosophy in Paris.

This professor, known for his quite dangerous opinions, previously made a trip to Germany several years ago; he then established close contact with scholars and professors in various German universities, and everything indicates that this trip was not without its political side. Because of these earlier events, I believe myself obliged to draw these two travellers to your particular attention.

Sincerely etc.
For the minister and by authorization:
FRANCHET-DESPEREY.
Director of Police.

Hoffmeister seems not to have been aware of this document. He only mentioned that the Prussian ambassador at Paris passed on to his own government Fanchet-Desperey's warning about the "danger" presented by Cousin's trip, but he does not specify that this warning had taken the form of an official note.[18]

In the normal course of events, the note would have been accompanied by oral comments, and the Prussian ambassador indicated that Franchet had given this warning "in confidence and in order to alert friendly courts." He recommended to his government not to make public the intervention of Franchet, and under no circumstances to mention the name of the French director of police.[19]

The Prussian rulers proceeded to gather information on Cousin. One of their double agents indicated that Cousin associated with some quite dangerous German "demagogues".

Without delay the minister, Count von Bernsdorff, ordered the arrest of Cousin in the event he enter Prussian territory. The Commission of Mainz was also alerted. On learning of Cousin's arrival at Dresden, it asked the Saxon government to have him apprehended. Cousin's arrest thus took place on the initiative of the French police, after consultation between the Commission of Mainz and the Saxon government and with the support of the Prussian government. Three governments against only one philosopher!

However, the Saxon government seems to have acted in this case against its real wishes, and only in order to obey the Commission of Mainz. It was not at all anxious to get further involved in the Cousin affair. On the other hand, Cousin's "accomplices", the German liberals with whom he was accused of "conspiring", were being charged by the Prussian police. The Saxon government washed its hands of Victor Cousin by turning him over to the Prussian government.

Cousin's incarceration in Berlin stretched on for three and a half months. After that, he had to remain in the Prussian capital under house arrest until 1825. The affair thus lasted for more than a year.

On a trip to Dresden, Hegel had met Cousin prior to his arrest. The two philosophers, who had known each other for some time, renewed their acquaintance with great pleasure, had long conversations, and visited common friends such as Böttiger. It is said that, on hearing of Cousin's arrest, Hegel was dumbfounded. He declared his conviction of his innocence, and immediately sent a long petition to the Prussian Minister of the Interior, in which he requested authorization to speak with the detainee and presented himself as a guarantor of his character and loyalty. This got nowhere.

Did Hegel act this way with full knowledge of the situation? Was Victor Cousin truly "innocent"?

"Only the stone is innocent," Hegel once wrote. Man becomes responsible — therefore guilty — as soon as he acts, because he cannot immediately realize the universal. Perhaps Hegel recalled his own doctrine when he took up his friend's defence. Cousin had lived, acted, and spoken: the police had evidence of his deeds and actions.

What motivated the director of the French police when he delivered to the Prussian ambassador the confidential note, fully aware that it would be taken seriously?

According to Georges Bourgin, the ministry then was "really" controlled by the *Congregation*.[20] And the same author points out that the *Congregation* took special interest in the top positions of the police:

> The *Society of Jesus* placed the French police in the hands of two of its associates by giving to Franchet-Desperey, a mere department head in the post office, general direction of the police, and to the counsellor of the Paris court, Delavau, the Prefecture of Police.[21]

These two men represented reaction in its most extreme form. They passionately persecuted all liberals, used questionable police methods, and were implacable in destroying "the hydra of the Revolution", which they saw reviving everywhere.

In particular they organized the surveillance and harassment of the Piedmontese revolutionary, Santa Rosa, with whom Cousin had formed a friendship. Under a false name Santa Rosa lived for a long time in Cousin's company at Auteuil, and it was there that the royal police arrested him. He could not be accused of anything specific, except for being who he was. So his prosecution was terminated. Nevertheless, the French police decided to expel him from French territory.

Victor Cousin, who had been associated with Santa Rosa since the latter's arrival in France, publicly took up his defence, intervening personally before the authorities, and had thus dealt directly with Delavau.[22]

Professor at the Sorbonne and at the Ecole Normale Supérieure, where he exercised a very great influence on young intellectuals, Cousin had been dismissed in 1820 for his liberal opinions and for the no less liberal character of his teaching. From that date, and even more after his encounter with Santa Rosa, the police watched him closely.

They evidently considered him to be one of the leaders of the liberal movement in intellectual circles. They would have liked to catch him red-handed and then get rid of him, but they were never successful. Taking account of the circumstances in France and of Cousin's popularity, they could hardly do more than "keep an eye on him."

It could very well be, then, that Franchet-Desperey hatched what was meant to be a Machiavellian plot. It can be easily reconstructed. We had the satisfaction of finding such an exposé in a study by Charles Bréville of *L'Arrestation de Cousin en Allemagne.* This author understood the mechanism of French police provocation very well, which he described thus:

> It is worth being quite clear about the French government's role. Cousin was one of those whom you dare not molest, whatever suspicions may surround them. Consequently—and the note of the French police, in the conditions in which it was sent, provides proof—advantage was taken of the double opportunity provided by Cousin's trip to Germany and by the occasion of Wit's denunciations to get the German police, who were not immediately concerned, to do a job that they could not have done by the French police. Villèle, who was the first and loudest to protest against the professor's arrest, certainly knew of Franchet's note, which, by the way, he never disclaimed. Having full control of the ministry of foreign affairs, there is no doubt that he would have severely punished anyone who took the liberty of sending a note to a foreign minister without first having it cleared.

> Does not this note, moreover, contain just before its signature the statement: "for the minister and by authorization," which, under the circumstances, one could not take to be a mere formula.[23]

We may add to these remarks of Bréville that the note, by simply naming a "Mister Cousin, professor of philosophy in Paris", hid from its addressees the notoriety of the person whom it denounced. Without doubt Franchet thought there would be no hesitation in Germany in arresting an insignificant and unknown professor; nor was he mistaken. He supposed further that Cousin was no more well known to the educated German public than to the Prussian police, and that in any case no German professor would dare speak up. However, on this point he was mistaken.

He imagined Cousin falling into the trap of the Berlin police; he relied on the Prussian judicial system to "grill" him in strict secrecy; it would be able to fabricate a plot sufficient to discredit Cousin publicly — or at least keep him behind bars for a long time.

At the moment of Cousin's arrest, the French chargé d'affaires in Dresden happened to be opportunely absent. An embassy employee, indignant at the treatment meted out to a French subject protected by a passport, judged it appropriate (the fool) to protest officially and to take several steps with the Saxon authorities. The first grain of sand in the gears...

At first the French government secretly disavowed to the Prussian and Saxon governments the inopportune steps taken by its representative in Dresden. Then, under the pressure of public opinion, and to calm the confusion of its agent, who could make neither head nor tail of the situation, the French government found itself obliged to shield him and to protest publicly in its own name against the arrest — which it had encouraged in secret. It then received a judicious response from a Saxon minister:

> the government of His Very Christian Majesty was no doubt not as displeased as it feigned to appear, and...the tone it took could be attributed only to the fear inspired in the Ministry by the next meeting of the Chamber of Deputies.[24]

Hegel's friend, the liberal Varnhagen, always well informed, noted in a letter of 1844 that the arrest of Cousin did not take place "according to quite vague suppositions, but rather upon the wish and instigation of the Paris secret police." He added that the French embassy in Dresden "took up the case of the accused only because of public opinion."[25]

Because the French government pretended to take up the defence of its national and condemned the proceedings of the Prussian police in order to hide the fact that they had incited them, relations quickly grew acrimonious between Paris and Berlin. The diplomats at first exchanged bittersweet words which then became vindictive. There was mutual distrust. The word *war* was even uttered.

The bad faith of the French government is striking and it is rather difficult to understand how Bréville, having cited Franchet's note and recounted the sordid manoeuvres of the French Minister of Foreign Affairs, could then reproach the Saxon government for its conduct toward Cousin. Throughout this whole affair, the Saxon government, acting simply as a tool for the designs of Franchet and the Prussian police, may be in fact the only one that was passively carried along as if compelled by circumstance.

It is unavoidable that we mention all these facts, if only briefly. For, outside of the official persons directly concerned, no man in Germany knew about them in more detail than did Hegel. After his release Cousin remained in Berlin under house arrest for a long time. During this period he had contact with several Prussian intellectuals, but in particular with his friend Hegel, with whom he had, from that time on, and later during the latter's trip to Paris, frequent, long and earnest conversations. It is inconceivable that he would not have recounted in detail to the friend who had come to his rescue the circumstances of his arrest and trial, the substance of the testimony against him, the course of the interrogation and so on.

Even if Hegel, so far as we know, never alluded in the writings he left us to the names of Franchet or Delavau, he nevertheless certainly knew of them. When in the *Lectures on the Philosophy of History*[26] he pointed out the credit due to the *Congregation* and the Baron von Eckstein for their study of the

Far East, he could not but have thought about the role that the *Congregation* had played in the Cousin affair. He could not have forgotten that the Baron von Eckstein, historiographer for the French Ministry of Foreign Affairs and fanatical partisan of the restoration and of ultramontanism, was also uncle of the agent provocateur, Witt-Döring[27], the main prosecution witness against Cousin. Here was an unavoidable association of names.

The Prussian police and courts could not have shown themselves more willing to perform the task suggested to them by Franchet's note. In seizing Victor Cousin, they believed that they had achieved a brilliant feat. They took the French philosopher to be a dangerous international agitator, closely linked to German revolutionaries, and working with them to incite a European uprising.

They had, indeed, just taken note of Witt-Döring's revelations, which exposed the subversive international secret societies and attested to Cousin's association with leaders of the *Burschenschaft* and of the German progressive movement — in particular with Follen, one of the more radical "demagogues", who was hated and feared the most.

Were they entirely mistaken?

In his usual way, after having summarized the events and provided a few documents, Hoffmeister says that,

> the entire course of the affair shows an excess of zeal on the part of the police and, to some extent, a lack of diplomatic skill on the part of the Prussian chargé d'affaires in Dresden.[28]

Like Ulrich and Carové, Asverus and von Henning, Cousin would also be an *innocent*, arrested in error! And in this case again, Hegel would have shown courage and friendship in intervening, but would not have thereby become politically involved.

Although incomplete, the documents published by Hoffmeister demonstrate quite well how valid were the charges against Cousin: he associated with German revolutionaries; in their company he reviewed the European political life and discussed measures for redirecting its course towards a liberal end.

It is certainly advisable to accept the declarations of double agents like Witt-Döring only with prudence. But he seems to have exhibited an intelligence and skill unusual for such a type. As well, he supported his denunciations with documents. Cousin could not avoid admitting many of the charges.

He had to allow that he had in fact met Professors Snell and Follen, in company with Witt, in Paris during the summer of 1820. He could not deny that he had met Snell again at Basel in 1821 while on a trip to Switzerland, a journey whose purpose remained obscure. He conceded, as well, that he knew the merchant and democrat, Liesching, from Stuttgart. In sum, on all the charges for which there was material evidence, Victor Cousin reluctantly had to confirm Witt's allegations.

He defended himself better overall when it came to the content and interpretation of the incriminating conversations. Even in this area, however, he sometimes found himself confronted by irrefutable documents. The investigators could, for example, present Cousin with a letter from Liesching to Snell, dated January 1821. It read:

> Several days ago Cousin was here. On their own the French will barely make it. But he is working diligently with several others; he has important connections. In company with such good men we will continue to promote the cause of the spirit of justice and truth.[29]

Cousin certainly tried to pass off these meetings with Snell, Follen, Liesching and Witt as inoffensive conversations, devoid of purpose and political content. But it was difficult to have this point of view prevail in the face of Witt's precise depositions and the documents that he produced.

Even the defence testimony that Baron von Eckstein agreed to give for some unknown reason in a letter to Witt backfired on Cousin. Eckstein confirmed the existence of a link between the French professor and Witt during the time the latter was passing for a liberal and revolutionary to better spy on the "conspirators". After this what weight could be given to Eckstein's assessment that Victor Cousin a few years previously "could well have dreamt and chattered a lot"?[30]

After examining Cousin's responses in the course of the interrogations, Bréville detected numerous contradictions and frequent, quite embarrassed admissions;[31] he even observed that on certain occasions, Cousin "completely foundered."[32] To get off the hook, the accused did not hesitate to lie and even accuse others whenever he thought the question involved circumstances or men about whom the Prussian police would not have first-hand information.[33] Bréville thought – and we are prepared to agree – that,

> despite his denials, Cousin's perfect acquaintance with the intrigues between Germans and French became more and more evident. Was not the Commission justified in believing that he had contributed to them?[34]

Of course the Prussian police – and its collusion with the French police is evident here as well – knew everything about Cousin's association with Santa Rosa and of the two men's difficulties with the French authorities.

Hoffmeister explained Cousin's ties to Santa Rosa in terms of the motives that Cousin himself later alleged, either publicly or in letters that he knew the police might eventually open: it was the nobility of heart and the human qualities of Santa Rosa that had aroused his friendship for the Piedmontese revolutionary.

Even such motives lead nonetheless to the most perilous of interpretations: the recognition of a great soul in a revolutionary leader proscribed and persecuted by the authorities was hardly the sort of sentiment that the authorities would share. The French and Prussian reactionaries had some difficulty in appreciating Santa Rosa's "fine feelings" or his "human qualities".

However, these motives were in fact combined with others. The friendship between Cousin and Santa Rosa took root because the two men shared the same liberal opinions. Birds of a feather flock together.

All the documents agree on this point: between 1820 and 1825 Cousin participated actively in the liberal movement, and he was certainly not unaware of the secret initiatives taken by European liberals, nor of their organisations, struggling against the Holy Alliance. More precisely, at this time Victor Cousin had very probably been a *carbonaro*.[35]

If Cousin was innocent in the eyes of history, he certainly was not according to the criteria of the Holy Alliance. The Prussian police had the best of reasons to believe that in truth – and to an extent that remained to be determined – Cousin "was conspiring" with German liberals.

An event soon took place that reinforced these suspicions and aggravated the plight of the accused. The Prussian government demanded the extradition of Follen and Snell, who had taken refuge in Switzerland some time earlier. The Swiss government refused. But scarcely had the news of Cousin's arrest become known than Follen and Wesselhöft[36] decided it would be wise to flee to America[37] – an indication of how directly affected they thought themselves to be. After Cousin's arrest, a European border no longer seemed to offer them sufficient protection from the machinations of the Prussian judicial system!

The flight of these two "demagogues" deprived the Prussian courts and police of two key witnesses. But in its own way it confirmed the accusations levelled against them and against Cousin.

Under these conditions we cannot agree with Hoffmeister's judgement:

> it appears that, on the whole, Hegel's conviction of Cousin's innocence of any revolutionary conspiracy was correct, and that the aggravating circumstances certainly testify to many interests and associations, but not to subversive activity strictly speaking.[38]

The definition of "subversive activity" varies with the person who gives it. The mere contact with men such as Follen, Snell, and Wesselhöft had often justified harsh sanctions against the members of the *Burschenschaft*. In the eyes of the Prussian courts, indeed, the case of Victor Cousin certainly raised more serious questions than those of Asverus or Ulrich, for example.

Did Hegel not question Cousin's innocence at all? He had known the latter since 1817, and Cousin many times affirmed that their friendship was based on political agreement. Their conversations regularly dealt with politics. Moreover, by his very close and constant association with members of the *Burschenschaft* and because of his interventions in numerous political trials, Hegel was well acquainted with the activity, goals, methods, and personalities of the German "demagogues". He had heard Follen and Snell spoken of frequently and at length, even if he did not know them personally. Wesselhöft was almost a member of the family.

The question asked by B. Knoop—even though he did not use all the documents we have just cited—is certainly not absurd:

> We may well ask if Hegel himself, with Cousin's assistance, did not want to realize some practical goals—in the domain of propaganda, for example.[39]

Hegel met Victor Cousin in Dresden. The two found each other without difficulty—as if each had been informed of the other's presence in the city. In his letters to his wife, Hegel generally gave all sorts of details about the friends encountered and the conversations held at the various stages of his journey. Yet Cousin, whose presence would be remarkable enough if it had been unforeseen, is not mentioned by name in the letters from Dresden. If the Cousin affair had not occurred, we probably would never have known anything about their conversations in Dresden.

In the course of his trial, Cousin declared that, in this city, he had only associated with "quite well known and respected people, such as Bodige and the Frenchman, Frédéric de Villers."[40] He too did not mention Hegel. But de Villers was a liberal. As for "Bodige", or Böttiger, Hegel's friend since 1820, we have here the German who, among his contemporaries, was without doubt the most knowledgeable about secret societies.

In fact, Hegel was so unsure of Cousin's "innocence"—and in addition there remained such uncertainty about what the police would be able to prove or not—that notwithstanding his courageous letter to the Minister of the Interior he took due precautions to provide an escape route in the event that Cousin was exposed. If one rereads with care this very thoroughly planned petition, one discovers that the author based his support for Cousin on their earlier association and on the evidence of fruitful scientific activity, but he carefully refrained from claiming anything concerning the eventual "innocence" of Cousin, leaving this point to be decided by the courts.[41]

Let us draw our conclusions. It may be true that at the moment of his arrest Cousin was not trying to realize any political project in Germany. Even then, his liberal convictions, which were going to receive a mortal blow from the trial itself, were becoming lukewarm. The fact remains: all the past deeds with which he was charged and upon which were grafted the present suspicions were genuine and testified against him.

In any event, Cousin did not immediately become conservative after the trial that contributed so much to his becoming demoralized had ended. Back in France, he became involved in erecting a monument to Santa Rosa on the Greek island where the latter had met his death while fighting for the cause he held dear. Like so many other European liberals, Santa Rosa had in fact joined one of those combat groups that came from all countries to aid the Greeks in their fight for independence. It was General Fabvier, commander of the corps of French volunteers, who undertook to erect the monument that Victor Cousin had dedicated to the memory of his friend.[42]

The Greece where Santa Rosa died, and where Cousin's associates fought, received support from the entire European intellectual community. All over — but particularly in Berlin — demonstrations in its favour developed into opposition movements against despotism. During this period Hegel visited an exhibition that his friend, the liberal bookseller Reimer, had organized "on behalf of the Greeks..."[43]

In arresting Cousin in 1824, the police of the Holy Alliance once more struck home; he was indeed one of their opponents whom they tried to reduce to submission.

One more time — what an inveterate habit — Hegel came to the rescue of a man who was, to say the least, eminently suspect.

3. The Group in Opposition

Hegel took an active interest in the fate of many of those who were accused. He was closely associated with the liberals of Berlin. Now these diverse relations could not be restricted to individuals in isolation. All of these men knew each other. Their shared ideals drew them together and made them one. They kept one another informed and supported one another. On occasion they belonged to the same societies, open or secret.

Even though there was no organization as such, there was a solidarity that effectively bound them together. They formed a movement of opinion, and constituted a particular political milieu. If somebody became associated with one of them, he thereby came into contact with a great number of like-minded men and heard all sorts of news about them.

Hegel knew intimately some of the student activists. The young Niethammer and Mrs. Hegel's brother, Gottlieb von Tucher, both members of the *Burschenschaft*, lived in the philosopher's own house where they were guests: this would mean daily contact, direct observation, and confidential conversations.

From the days in Heidelberg on, his favorite disciple, Carové, met with Hegel nearly every day. We know that Hegel did not enjoy talking about his philosophical system in private conversation. But he nevertheless knew how to take his part in the latter. He would chat at length, and politics would be the main theme.

He was no less intimate with Förster: the two men took long walks and excursions together. Förster's interests focused essentially on national and political problems.

In Hegel's last years, Gans as well visited him every day to discuss the latest news.[44] And for his part, Cousin has recalled the long afternoons spent chatting with Hegel, comfortably settled on a sofa.

Each of these friends of Hegel would speak with him about the others, as well as about their close associates.

Asverus was regularly in the company of Niethammer and Gottlieb von Tucher, as well as Carové. He was well acquainted with some of the key leaders of the *Burschenschaft*, such as Loholm, Kobbe, Roediger (one of the organizers of the *Wartburg* demonstration), and Gustav Jung. Friedrich Förster and the bookseller Reimer were among his close associates.

Carové dealt with nearly all the important members of the *Burschenschaft*: Follen, Roediger, Jung and Ackermann, in his role as organizer; and as a student of Hegel, with all of the latter's disciples. Of his closest friends let us simply mention von Henning, Hinrichs, Görres (whom he was to see during his exile in Strassbourg), Förster, Victor Cousin, Walter, and Creuzer.

Victor Cousin had connections with Fries, Reimer, Gans, Förster, Follen, Snell, Witt-Döring, with many Italian liberals (Rossi, Santa Rosa, Salfi, Prati), and with almost all the French liberals: Thiers, Mignet, Fauriel, Royer-Collard, the editors of the *Constitutionnel* and of the *Globe*, and so on.

Indeed, strange though it may seem, it appears that his circle of acquaintances included figures of whom the young Hegel had certainly heard, such as the famous Count von Schlabrendorff, at whose home Follen probably had his first encounter with Witt, before they made contact with Cousin.[45] In earlier days he had welcomed to Paris nearly all the Germans favourable to the French Revolution, among them Oelsner, whom Hegel admired.[46] *

Curiously, Gans also met Oelsner. During the course of a trip to Paris, he visited Benjamin Constant. He had connections with Heine and, like Carové, took an interest in the Saint-Simonian movement.

It would be impossible to draw up a list of all the personalities who were progressive, liberal, revolutionary, or suspected by the authorities, and with whom the friends and disciples of Hegel maintained cordial, and sometimes very close, relations. The few preceding examples suffice, we believe, to show that they were quite numerous and varied, in many settings and in several countries. Thanks to them, Hegel was certainly one of the best informed men in Germany about what was happening in the liberal camp.

In the judicial inquiries which Hegel followed the most closely, these persons usually found themselves implicated in groups, judged and condemned together, confronted with, and invited to testify against, each other. This happened with Carové, von Henning, and Asverus. And in 1824, the Berlin judges issued simultaneous warrants for the arrest of Cousin, Snell, Follen, Wesselhöft, and others.

In fact it was with a group of those in opposition that Hegel was linked. But that does not mean they were all in constant and complete agreement among themselves. For example, until a final truce was reached, Asverus, Niethammer, and von Tucher opposed violently and at length "that cowardly son of a bitch Carové", who wanted the *Burschenschaft* to accept Jews into its ranks.[47]

During the course of police investigation, one of them might on occasion let himself go and criticise the others. Thus, some of the accused made statements in which they reproached Carové for having too soft an attitude, a lack of militancy against the government. This could have been a move of self-denial, in which they accused themselves so that their accomplice would be helped. This small circle of intellectuals, eager for political renewal, was lively, contradictory, and complex. Hegel watched it evolve, expand, and become mature; but prior to his death he could not have noticed within Germany any increase in its power and influence. It remained weak and impoverished; one by one its efforts, seemingly so ridiculous, were crushed by the powerful of this world.

4. The Masters of the World

It is worth stressing a significant feature of the judicial inquiries that preoccupied Hegel. As we have seen, they were essentially about crimes of intention, which found expression in trivial acts: a student cried "Long live Jahn!"; a professor published a journal article in which he accused the court of carrying on intrigues against the king and people; a foreign philosopher seemed to weave a plot with three or four German liberals, which, if genuine, would have presented absolutely no danger to the state . . .

These were the minor offences of academics, most of whom were certainly not lacking in status, but whose coalition remained extremely feeble. And to suppress these crimes, an enormous mobilization of police forces, with the most exalted personalities of the State at their head!

Leafing through the accounts of the Förster and Cousin affairs, or even of those wretched trials of mere students, Ulrich or Asverus, we discover that it was not regular judges who conducted them, and assumed responsibility for their outcome.

Astonishingly, we find the director of the Prussian police, von Kamptz himself, studying the dossier of Asverus in minute detail and constantly intervening in the course of the investigations and trial. For this minor affair, which involved duelling by a member of the *Burschenschaft*, the commission of inquiry did not hesitate to send reports directly to the Minister of the Interior, who not only read them, but examined them and responded in his own hand.

Asverus' parents, subjects of the Duke of Saxe-Weimar, prevailed upon their government to take diplomatic action on behalf of their son. The chargé d'affaires of Saxe-Weimar handed to Hardenberg a note from his Minister of Foreign Affairs concerning ... Asverus!

As his trial dragged on intolerably, the latter had no other course than to petition the King of Prussia directly, who for his part wrote personally to Hardenberg concerning the matter, informed himself at first hand, studied the question with great care, and delivered a final decree.

At the end of his ordeal, Asverus could at least take pride in having received the attentions of two chiefs of state, a king and a duke, two ministerial councils, that of Saxe-Weimar and that of Prussia, and a great number of ministers who had to intervene personally.

Altenstein, Hardenberg and von Kamptz exchanged extensive correspondence concerning Ulrich. Carové provoked the direct intervention of the Great Chamberlain and Minister of State, his Highness the Prince of Sayn and Wittgenstein. This time the initiative came from above: it shook the Minister of Public Instruction, Altenstein, who was aimed at indirectly, as well as his protector, Chancellor Hardenberg; it moved the Ministers von Kircheisen and von Schuckmann to action, and of course von Kamptz, who took part in each of these festivities.

The Förster affair involved the same key figures: the King, the court and the ministers. But it was a military matter; it also involved the Minister of War, the members of the court-martial, General von Lilienstern, and so on — not counting, once again, the government of Saxe-Weimar.

Cousin broke all records. Three or four governments, several sovereigns, some directors of national police, a great number of diplomats and officers, not counting a whole army of police, spies and stool pigeons, devoted a good part of their time and activity to him for weeks on end.

The rulers of Prussia consulted every file, examined documents, and read confiscated letters. They scrutinized the associations of Asverus, Förster, Carové and Cousin, as well as of other accused, and each time they came across the name of ... Hegel!

The "philosopher of the State" did indeed stick his nose into many of the affairs of the State. But did this indiscretion always please the masters of his country?

5. The Results of Hegel's Interventions

One of the most frequent theories, albeit for Hegel the most injurious, is that Hegel, in his interventions, conformed to the initiatives of the reactionary party in government, that he followed the wishes of the police and sought to achieve their ends.

Hegel is supposed to have intervened, not to defend the accused, but rather to "pacify" them: to turn them from their original opinions, and convert them to the policies of absolute monarchy. He is said to have devoted himself to the task of demoralizing the members of the opposition, the proof being that under his influence they are all supposed to have finally "toed the line".

Two categories of evidence refute such allegations in their entirety. The first relates to the success of Hegel's efforts; the second, to the later attitudes of the accused.

Asverus's case gives us an opportunity to assess the kind of results that Hegel could hope to obtain by the resolute and insistent steps he took.

Upon the arrest of this student, Hegel undertook to forward to the police a message from his father, enclosed in a letter from his own hand supporting the accused.[48] From then on he remained constantly in touch with the detainee, his father and his lawyer, unstintingly offering advice, taking new initiatives, and keeping up on developments through direct contact with the chief of police, von Kamptz.

Soon he was entering into negotiations with the commission of inquiry, going to the court house himself to secure Asverus's release on bail. He offered himself as a guarantor that Asverus would continue to remain at the court's disposition during the investigation.[49]

An arrangement of this sort was finally achieved and, after a long detention, the prisoner was released directly into the hands of Hegel, who had supplied bail amounting to 500 thalers guaranteeing Asverus's promise to abstain from all objectionable comments about his incarceration, to get promptly well away from Berlin, and to remain at the disposition of the authorities.[50]

The bail paid by Hegel was not returned until 1823 when he obtained, not its cancellation, but only its transformation into a right to garnishee his wages.[51]

Recall that Asverus's trial lasted until November 1826!

Hegel did not hesitate to sacrifice himself; the facts speak for themselves. But to such small effect! When we take account of how weak the accusations against Asverus were, and what was the offence he actually committed, we may well imagine that, even without Hegel's aid and even without the diplomatic steps taken by Saxe-Weimar, the accused could have scarcely remained longer in preventive detention, that his trial could hardly have dragged on for much longer, nor could it have concluded differently.

Indeed, it is quite incredible that such a heavy punishment (six years in prison) was inflicted upon him in the first instance and that the King waited more than seven years to close the case.

To put it bluntly, we have the impression that the intervention of the government of Saxe-Weimar as well as that of Hegel served instead as *aggravating* circumstances.

In any case, it does not appear that Hegel conducted himself according to the wishes of the Prussian government and its police. In what way could he have been serving them in this affair? He was obviously working to assist Asverus, not his persecutors.

The substance and outcome of the Carové and von Henning affairs rule out even more definitively, if that is possible, any thought of collusion between Hegel and the police. In fact he was himself targeted at the same time as his assistants. In both cases his efforts to assist them ended in failure. Carové's career was destroyed; Henning remained in preventive custody for a long time, even though the prosecution was based on ridiculous pretexts.

It may be that Hegel had greater success in helping Förster. It could have been due to him that the latter was reinstated in the administration, five years after his suspension.

In our opinion, there was no case in which Hegel showed himself more effective than in that of Cousin—but not in the way one usually understands that term.

In his *Life of Hegel*, after summarizing the French professor's German adventure, Rosenkranz credited Hegel with having had a part in Cousin's release. He reproduced a passage from Hegel's letter to the Minister of the Interior, and added:

> On the basis of this intervention, the mediation of the French ambassador and his own word of honour, Cousin was set free. He stayed a bit longer in Berlin where he remained in an amicable and philosophically fruitful contact with Hegel and some of his students: Gans, Hotho, von Henning and Michelet.[52]

The documents provide evidence that almost all of this is false. Hegel's letter to the Minister of the Interior had *no* positive results; his request to visit the prisoner was rejected. The "mediation" of the French embassy on behalf of Cousin, coming after Franchet's initiative, produced at first *no* results, and when it became insistent provoked irritation. It almost precipitated a diplomatic incident. After his release, Cousin certainly remained in Berlin, but Rosenkranz forgot to specify that he was forced to remain there, under surveillance! Of Rosenkranz's statements there remain only the possibility of Cousin's word of honour, and the certainty of Hegel's friendship and that of his disciples.

It is quite false to say that Hegel succeeded in having Cousin released through his "influence" with the Prussian government or his "good relations" with the police. Cousin's detention extended over a long period; the inquiry was pursued with severity; and Hegel was not able to obtain directly any alleviation of this. He was only too happy not to be himself an object of suspicion and harassment.

We have said, however, that Hegel's letter was useful. How so?

Recall the conditions under which the inquiry ended. The judgment of the Commission of Mainz that was forwarded on February 22, 1825 to the French ambassador at the German Diet, Reinhard, spelled them out quite clearly. It stated:

> 1st, that there had been sufficient cause to request the arrest; 2nd, that it appeared from the trial evidence that Mr. Cousin could not be entirely cleared of the serious charges that had been brought; 3rd, that he would nevertheless be released.[53]

One could hardly put things better: if Cousin had been set free, it was not at all because his innocence was recognized, but for other reasons. In spite of numerous appeals, moreover, the Prussian Minister ever after refused to attest to Cousin's innocence.

In our view, there are three factors, of differing status, which should be considered when explaining the French professor's ultimate release.

First of all, there was a lack of coordination between the different police forces, and inadequate preparation for the dirty work. Doubtless the three police forces, French, Prussian and Saxon, wanted nothing more than to co-operate. But even though their intentions converged, their political situations were not the same. The police forces acted within their own national settings, each one different from the others. Everything would have gone well had not the public in each country learned of what was happening next door. However, Cousin's arrest at Dresden had already provoked something of a demonstration locally, thanks to the lively reactions of the Duke of Montebello. In the final analysis, each police force had agreed to bring Cousin to heel on condition that the police force of another country would accept responsibility for the operation. United against the liberals, the Holy Alliance broke apart as soon as the governments wanted to appear as representing the national interest in the eyes of their own people. Remarkably enough, during the entire course of the operations the Ministers of Foreign Affairs turned out to be the most reticent. In particular, if he had not been explicitly obliged to obey orders from above, the Saxon minister would have willingly nipped the affair in the bud.[54]

It was those in charge of the lowly police, Franchet-Desperey in France and Schuckmann in Berlin, who initiated and directed the operation. But they required the cooperation of men who did not have, as they did, the experience and the taste for agents provocateurs, double-dealing and back rooms. Witt-Doring, the "double agent" (as Reinhardt[55] called him), did not arouse sympathy everywhere. In addition, some naive individuals were taken in and wondered whether this provocateur was in fact an actual revolutionary!

Cousin's accusers lacked adequate witnesses. If to their mind the flight of Snell, Follen and Wesselhöft encouraged and confirmed the accusations, it nevertheless removed the possibility of objective confirmation. The absence of these witnesses – or accomplices – and the certainty that there was no threat of being confronted with them, made it easier for Cousin to plead his case.

This leads to the second point: Cousin defended himself well. The fact that he was kept in solitary confinement explains some blunders. But on the whole, he was skilful in knowing how to use the circumstances whose existence and contours were progressively revealed to him in the course of the interrogations. In the end, there was only one witness against him, Witt-Döring, dangerous because he knew nearly everything, but whose dishonesty none could question.

At first Cousin denied everything outright. Then he little by little had to admit whatever the documents proved, but nothing more. Schuckmann finally had to acknowledge the success of this tactic:

> In his declaration of the 10th of this month, Cousin was in no way able to destroy the strong suspicions raised against him by Dewitt. In truth, Cousin admitted to his intimate relationship with Follenius and his contacts with him up to the matter in question, and whatever was easy to prove, but he denied in a most formal way any link with him on the subject we wanted to clarify.[56]

It may be that account must also be taken of the monarchist pronouncements and avowals of allegiance to the king that Cousin sent France from his prison, each of which became to the French reaction a pledge for the future. If these do in part explain Cousin's later behaviour in France, however, they would have exercised only a minimal, or even a negative, influence on the Prussian government's final decision.

What forced the latter to give up in the end was public opinion. It was a factor from the beginning and gave the affair the kind of publicity that its promoters wished to avoid.

But one must mention how timid it was at first.

It was originally sparked by the inopportune zeal of the ill-informed embassy official in Dresden, as well as by the courageous reaction of the Duke of Montebello.

Subsequently protests spread, in tandem with the sensational news, throughout the liberal circles of Europe. Yet at first the protests remained very discreet in Prussia. Fear kept all lips sealed.

In his account of Victor Cousin's arrest, Eugène Spuller wrote that on this occasion

all the Prussian liberals were devoted in giving him evidence of a most sympathetic interest.[57]

In reality the "Prussian liberals" showed hardly any support for Cousin *until after he was released*! One cannot blame them; they were weighed down by constant surveillance, a permanent threat.

All the same, Prussian public opinion did find expression. And Hegel was its voice. By his letter the authorities learned that, even in Prussia, there were people who knew Cousin, held him in high esteem and were disturbed by his situation. Hegel's gesture quickly became known. The authorities took account of it, but in no way as an act of servility: it is difficult to see how it could ever have appeared so to them.

They took Hegel's letter as indicating the "temperature" of public opinion and of the repercussions of Cousin's arrest in their own country; they realized that they should not proceed too brutally or thoughtlessly, and that it was advisable not to "go too far".

Incidents such as Hegel's letter thwarted in particular the motives of Franchet-Desperey, who had hoped that there, far from Paris, Cousin's fate would be settled with the utmost discretion. Prudent though the letter was, it proclaimed in its own way the solidarity of the "republic of letters" in regard to one of its own, and at the same time it dared to show the affection of a Berlin philosopher for a publicly declared liberal.

Hegel, who had on occasion exhibited some contempt for public opinion, thus became its eminent representative in dangerous circumstances: its eminent representative and, note well, the *only* one in Prussia.

Because of the protests raised all over Europe and the malaise that emerged even in Prussia, from the evidence of Hegel's letter, it soon became evident that the Cousin affair was doing more to harm those who had set it in motion than it brought them benefit. And they decided to put an end to it.

The head of the Holy Alliance, Metternich himself, was the first to see the danger. He intervened with the Commission of Mainz to have the inquest concluded as quickly as possible.[58] His seconds in each country, and Schuckmann in particular, followed in his footsteps. So Cousin was released.

In this case we see that Hegel's success was unambiguous. There is here no submission by the philosopher to the whims of power, no servility or compliance. Hegel showed himself to be a friend who flew to the aid of his friend, an imprisoned liberal whose case alarmed all his other liberal friends as well as all of liberal Europe. Because this European liberal movement existed, Hegel's feeble voice gained in strength and, in concert with others, ended by making itself heard.

This examination of the various cases, political and judicial, exonerates Hegel of the misdeeds with which he is to this day charged. Think only, for example, of P. Reimann's assertion:

> The reactionary role that Hegel played in the political life of his time, found expression in his *Philosophy of Right* as well as *in his attacks on the student movement*, confused and influenced by romantic tendencies though it was, which, despite all its weaknesses, was the first expression of any opinions that opposed the system of the 'Holy Alliance'.[59]

Upon what documents does Schnabel base his peremptory assertion with respect to the Prussian repression of "demagogic intrigues" that during all of this campaign Hegel obstinately (*unentwegt*!) took the side of the authority and reasons of State.[60]

6. The Persecuted Testify

Far from "denouncing" the liberals to the police, or aiding the latter in their attempts at repression, Hegel was, as we have seen, something of a nuisance to the authorities. But did he not, nevertheless court their favour by offering the rebels, the detainees and the suspects a kind of conservative political propaganda?

He is accused of having worked to "pacify" turbulent youths, of having transformed rebels into lambs, and of having brought members of the opposition to an attitude of submission. Altenstein defended Hegel from his enemies by claiming that the philosopher

was decidedly opposed in every possible way to the anarchy that reigned among the young people.[61]

Hegel was certainly not much taken with the excesses of certain members of the *Burschenschaft*: their old-German costume, their complaining, and above all their fanatical mania for duelling. But is all this really so revolutionary? Should we blame Hegel for attacking it and for trying to convince his friends to take more reasonable attitudes?

After several years in contact with Hegel, Asverus expressed opinions that Hoffmeister regarded as more "moderate".[62] But what "extremism" does this moderation attenuate? In fact, through contact with Hegel, Asverus's xenophobia and anti-semitism was tempered, something we cannot regret. The young man was now more interested in theoretical and philosophical problems. Yet he remained true to his ideal of "freedom" and the "unity of the nation".[63] He now simply translated his ideas into Hegelian terms, without letting the orientation of his political and patriotic convictions waver.

As for Carové, he did not come "into line". All his life he remained true to himself, without renouncing his admiration for Hegel nor breaking off friendly relations with his teacher. He translated French authors into German. The choice betrays his own leanings: Victor Cousin, Benjamin Constant, Diderot, Royer-Collard, Sismondi, and Stendhal.

The article in the *Allgemeinen Deutschen Biographie* on Friedrich Förster suggests that,

> under Hegel's influence a perceptible change was produced in his political attitude, which turned him away from his utopian dreams for the betterment of the world and from his juvenile enthusiasm for freedom towards new and loftier goals. As a result the king's favour was again bestowed on him, and he was named curator of the art gallery.

Are we to reproach Förster for having tried to get another administrative post after his dismissal? We would then seem rather severe towards him. After all, no one dreams of rebuking the German revolutionary, Rebmann, for having ended his life as a state judge in Bavaria.[64]

Here as well Förster's "pacification" could have very well involved early tendencies that were hardly progressive in themselves. He did not become reactionary. We shall soon recall his progressive declarations at Hegel's funeral.

Hegel contributed to the rejection of Teutonism, xenophobia, anti-semitism, anarchistic individualism, and vainly provocative rhetoric. But he did not thereby reconcile his students with absolutism, arbitrary power, the Holy Alliance, or German particularism.

Some of Hegel's protégés, it is true, became "turncoats": von Henning and Victor Cousin, for example.

In the judgement of Varnhagen, von Henning became a "zealous servant" of all governments. But one must consider the dates and the correlations. Von Henning entered the reactionary camp after Eichhorn had succeeded Altenstein; but, even more significant for our purposes, he abandoned Hegelianism at the same time.[65] This coincidence, far from testifying to the reactionary character of Hegelian philosophy, serves rather to show that it was difficult to be subservient while remaining Hegelian.

Victor Cousin as well changed his political attitude only after his detention in Berlin, perhaps under its influence. "M. Cousin did not enjoy playing the martyr," said Spuller.[66] However, the shift in his political convictions did not happen right away, or all at once. Cousin took the time to erect the monument to the memory of Santa Rosa that we mentioned; and he continued to frequent liberal circles in Paris.

And there again, the disaffection with progressive ideas accompanied a renunciation of Hegelianism. Even before that, Victor Cousin had deplored Hegel's attachment to the *philosophes* of the 18th century.

When politically he turned away from liberalism, he drew philosophically nearer to Schelling; and after Hegel's death he stressed this conversion at the time when Schelling came to Berlin to combat a Hegelianism that everyone, from then on, took as the principal ideological adversary of reaction.

On the other hand, Gans remained true to his ideas in the political, as well as the philosophical, realm. To the end he was Hegel's committed disciple; and at the same time his political attitude earned him, more and more, the hatred of the feudal class.

Whatever their subsequent destiny might be, none of these men submitted in any way at all to the government's wishes while Hegel knew and supported them. They belonged to the opposition; for this reason they were attacked.

Better than anyone else, they knew Hegel's leanings; in addition, because of their situation, they more than others had the right to judge him.

None of them either blamed or criticised Hegel. All of them, even those such as Cousin and Henning who later abandoned Hegelianism, expressed the greatest respect for, and complete confidence in him. It never occurred to them, and for good reason, that Hegel had wanted to dupe them, that he had not been their sincere friend, or that the sympathy shown them had not extended to their behaviour and ideas.

Conservatism? Reaction? Traces of such have been looked for in the *Philosophy of Right*, particularly after the death of its author.

But the "demagogues" to whose aid he went and with whom he met daily did not detect them in his conduct, in his writings or in his statements.

Yet some did not show any indulgence at all towards their adversaries — or even towards their luke-warm friends. They were quick to put others on the spot; they did not hesitate to style as traitorous or faint-hearted those who appeared not to act in entire conformity with their views, unorthodox though they often were. But they respected Hegel.

Thus Asverus, who in his letters was so profuse in showering insults on his own companions, on Schleiermacher and on the Berlin professors in general, and who, it must be admitted, vented his ill-temper on just about everyone, nonetheless wrote to his friend Gabler:

> The professors here, at least for the most part, are spineless servants, except perhaps for Hasse, Hegel and de Wette.[67]

Moreover, this compromising appraisal of Hegel fell into the hands of the police.

Asverus also recounted in a letter how Hegel had taken part in a student festival:

> On the 18th we went to Treptow, in the company of several professors, among whom were Hegel, Hasse, Savigny, Göschen, with musical accompaniment. There we ate and drank, led cheers and talked quite a bit; unfortunately, this was not done publicly, that is to say, no one came forward to give a speech.[68]

We see here that Asverus certainly considered Hegel to be a "sympathizer".

Had he not already taken part in the Pichelsberg festival on May 2, 1819? Eighty-six members of the *Burschenschaft* got together on this occasion. As far as professors were concerned, there were only Schleiermacher, de Wette and Hegel. The political character of this demonstration was undeniable. Frederick Förster delivered a speech on Kotzebue's death, which was similar in inspiration to Carové's pamphlet, itself patterned overall on Hegel's ideas. He said:

> We will not drink to the glory of Sand; but we wish that evil would fall without the need for the stab of a dagger.[69]

It seems that this festival did not provoke a judicial reaction.

Hegel was also invited to the "Armament Festival", organized in honour of the decree concerning universal conscription. He gave his assent, but then, Hoffmeister tells us (unfortunately without being more precise), he found himself led (*bewogen*) to reverse his decision and to refrain from attending the festival in order to avoid raising false suspicions.[70]

We rather believe that Hegel had well-founded suspicions. The students regularly invited him to their demonstrations, and he refrained from showing up only when he had been warned about an imminent danger.

If he "pacified" some of their fanciful goals, he encouraged other, more serious ones. In 1826, L. Geiger tells us,

> Hegel drank with the students a toast to the storming of the Bastille; he said he never failed to do it each year, and endeavoured to make clear to the young people how significant this event was.[71]

Cousin sent Hegel repeated expressions of his gratitude for the courage shown during his detention.[72] Much later, at a time when he was not at all inclined to recall his youthful convictions, Cousin portrayed Hegel's political attitude at Berlin this way:

> In politics, M. Hegel is the only man from Germany with whom I was always on the best of terms. He was, like me, infused with the new spirit; he considered the French Revolution to be the greatest step forward taken by humankind since Christianity and he never ceased questioning me about the issues and men of this great epoch. He was profoundly liberal without being the least bit republican.[73]

And in 1866 Cousin was without doubt glossing over the truth of 1824....

As for Förster, at the graveside of his master he delivered a speech somewhat disorganized, but obviously sincere. He composed the eulogy for the philosopher who had just passed away and, sensing the enemies of Hegelianism at work all around, he affirmed that the memory of his master would be resolutely defended. This is the way he apostrophized Hegel's opponents:

> Draw near, Pharisees and Scribes, who arrogantly and ignorantly misunderstand and malign him. We will know how to defend his fame and his honour! Draw near, stupidity, foolishness, cowardice, apostasy, hypocrisy, and fanaticism! Draw near, servile sentiments

and obscurantism. We are not afraid of you, because his spirit will be our guide![74]

And in fact it was against servility and obscurantism that the Hegelians soon had to defend Hegel's memory.

NOTES

1. *Briefe,* III, 374-378.

2. G. Weill, *L'Eveil des nationalités*, (Paris, 1930) 47.

3. The expression is an echo of Hegel's: "World history is the final judgement." [and of a dictum of Schiller's which Hegel himself appropriated — the Oxford Dictionary of Quotations says "First lecture as Professor of History, 26 May, 1789"]

4. *Briefe*, II, 271-272; *Letters,* 470.

5. See Hoffmeister's note, *Briefe*, II, 482.

6. Ibid, 504.

7. Ibid, 436, note by Hoffmeister.

8. *Briefe*, III, 365. Note by Hoffmeister.

9. Ibid, 24-25; *Letters*, 472.

10. See *Briefe*, II, 440-441.

11. Ibid.

12. *Briefe*, II 499.

13. This refers to a young member of the *Burschenschaft*.

14. Cited by Hoffmeister, *Briefe*, II, 459.

15. *Briefe*, II, 458.

16. Ibid. 461.

17. See *Briefe*, II, 468, notes.

18. *Briefe*, III, 375, notes.

19. Ibid.

20. In the restoration period in France a number of conservative Catholic laymen formed the *Congregation of the Faith,* which was suspected of reactionary tendencies and of close association with the Jesuits. [translators' note]

21. G. Bourgin, "Cousin et Santa Rosa," *Revue historique*, vol. 103, (1910), 311.

22. Paul-Louis Courier, as well, had resided with Victor Cousin during his court case in 1821. We know that the pamphleteer was condemned to two months in prison.

23. C. Bréville, *L'Arrestation de Victor Cousin en Allemagne (1824-1825)*, (offprint of the *Nouvelle Revue de Paris*), Paris, 1910, 55.

24. Cited by Bréville, *op.cit.* 32-33.

25. Cited by Hoffmeister, *Briefe*, III, 376, notes.

26. The reference is to the French translation by Gibelin, pp. 60-61n2.

27. He is also referred to under the names: Witt, Wit, de Witt, Dewitt, Döring, etc. A double agent with many names...

28. *Briefe*, III, 375.

29. See *Briefe* III, 376, notes of Hoffmeister.

30. Ibid.

31. Bréville, *op.cit.*, 38.

32. Ibid. 41.

33. Bréville, *op.cit.*, 39-40 and 45.

34. Ibid. 42.

35. See Thureau-Dangin, *Le Parti libéral sous la Restauration*. (Paris, 1876) 112 and 233-236. See also C. Bréville, *op.cit.* 55: "The Carbonaro of 1824...."

36. On Wesselhöft, see above, pp 113ff.

37. See *Briefe* III, 377, note of Hoffmeister.

38. Ibid.

39. B. Knoop, *V. Cousin, Hegel und die französische Romantik*, (Berlin, 1932) 43n12.

40. Bréville, *op.cit.*, 7.

41. See *Briefe*, III, 77; *Letters*, 635.

42. G. Bourgin, *op.cit.*, 86-87.

43. *Briefe* III, 120, and note, p. 399.

44. Karl Hegel, *Leben und Erinnerungen*, p. 10.

45. Bréville, *op.cit.*, p. 34.

46. See my *Hegel Secret*, Part I, Chapter 1.

47. "*Der Dumme Hundsfott Carové*" (Asverus *scripsit*, *Briefe*, II, p. 433.)

48. *Briefe II*, pp. 216-217; *Letters*, 449.

49. Ibid. 439-440, notes.

50. Ibid. 440.

51. Ibid. III, 14-15; *Letters*, 451-2.

52. Rosenkranz, *op.cit.*, p. 369.

53. Cited by Bréville, *op.cit.*, 52.

54. See Bréville, *op.cit.*, 14-15.

55. See Bréville, *op.cit.* 54. On Reinhardt see my study: *Hegel secret*, Part I, Chapter 1.

56. Cited by Bréville, 53.

57. E. Spuller, *Figures disparues*, 70.

58. Bréville, *op.cit.* 52.

59. P. Reimann, *Hauptströmung der deutschen Literatur 1750-1848*, Berlin 1956, 533. Italics are mine.

60. F. Schnabel, *Deutsche Geschichte im Neunzehnten Jahrhundert*, Bd. II, Freiburg 1949, p. 261.

61. *Briefe*, II, 466.

62. *Briefe*, II, 434.

63. *Briefe*, II, 436.

64. See E. Vögt, *Die deutsche jakobinische Literatur*, Berlin, 1955.

65. See Hegel, *Berliner Schriften*, Hoffmeister's note, p. 607.

66. Spuller, *op.cit.* 80-81.

67. *Briefe*, II, 435n.

68. Ibid. 436.

69. See *Briefe*, IV, 175-176.

70. Ibid.

71. L. Geiger, *Berlin, 1688-1840*. Berlin, 1895, II, 545.

72. See *Briefe*, III, 404-405.

73. *Revue des Deux Mondes*, 1866, 616-617.

74. Rosenkranz, *Hegels Leben*, 566.

IV

The Clandestine Hegel

1. Daring and Caution

The *young Hegelians* who undertook to continue Hegel's work after his death did not know everything about his many judicial interventions, compromising as they were. Not yet public were the police archives that now document them for us. Direct witnesses were passing away, as did Gans, or were deserting the Hegelian camp, as did Cousin and Henning. Those who were constant remained silent because the persecution of opposition became more pointed.

One aspect of Hegel's life, perhaps the most important, risked falling into oblivion.

Fortunately, the police were vigilant.

Their evil intentions were more efficient than the piety of the disciples. They carefully filed away the traces of Hegel's actions that have allowed us to rehabilitate him.

They saved the philosopher's honour in the judgement of history, because they wanted to ruin him in the eyes of an ephemeral Holy Alliance. The thinker of the dialectic would have loved such an "inversion".

* * * * * * * * *

But the police did not keep an eye on all aspects of Hegel's existence. He was not kept constantly under observation. A few deeds, a few statements and a few letters escaped them.

Evidence of diverse sorts opens up for us a side of Hegel's life that agents from the Ministry of the Interior could not scrutinize. But naturally the philosopher did not take the trouble to spell out for us what he wanted to hide from ill-disposed contemporaries. We therefore have to deal with fragmentary clues: less with documents as such than with the traces left when they were destroyed.

We need not imagine an unceasing underground activity, wide-reaching and productive. Some vestige of such action would have survived to our day; or at least the police would have found it out.

Given the political conditions of the time, with the progressive movement weak and isolated among the German people, no wide-spread illegal activity was possible. Hegel did not think of taking on the vested authorities in a head-on collision; his political thought did not move towards such firm convictions. He was no revolutionary.

Nevertheless, several escapades, a few infractions of the law and its regulations, some evidence of a reluctance to conform and one or two signs of insubordination can be added to the sum of his interventions with the courts and police (legal even though in opposition), to his expressions of friendship for the "demagogues", and to all that was bold in his theories. The resulting sketch is of quite a different personality from the one that Lucien Herr once described in these terms:

> Throughout his life Hegel remained a man of pure intellect, lacking a public life; a man of powerful internal imagination, neither charming nor congenial; a member of the middle class with modest and drab virtues; above all, he was an official, intimate with law and order, realistic and subservient.[1]

Rosenkranz, in his *Life of Hegel* published in 1844, gives us an example of Hegel's "respect" for "law and order" at a time when the Prussian government was repressing dissent with the greatest brutality. His story does not lack piquancy:

> Hegel's generosity (says Rosenkranz) let itself be drawn to the limits of the fantastic. We will offer only one small example. Because of his political contacts one of his auditors[2] found himself in the bailiff's prison, which backed on the River Spree. Friends of the detainee made contact with him, and because they rightly considered him innocent, as indeed the trial showed, they sought to demonstrate their solidarity by sailing in a boat under the window of his cell at midnight and trying to talk with him. The attempt had succeeded once already, and the friends, also Hegel's auditors, managed to tell him about the affair in such a way that he too decided to participate

in the expedition. The bullet of one sentinel could very well have saved the converter of demagogues from any further tribulations! It also seems that, on the water, Hegel was seized with a sense of how strange the situation was. In effect, once the boat stopped before the window, the exchange was to begin; as a precaution it was to take place in Latin. But Hegel limited himself to a few innocent generalities asking the prisoner, for example: "Num me vides?" Since he was almost at arm's length, the question was somewhat comical, and it did not fail to provoke a great deal of laughter, in which Hegel joined with much Socratic banter on the return trip.[3]

In this text, Rosenkranz gives us both a fact and its interpretation. But does the interpretation agree with the fact?

Let us distinguish between them.

First of all, the fact: the Professor of Philosophy of the University of Berlin prowls in the company of "demagogic" students, in a boat, at midnight, at the foot of the walls of the state prison, and enters into contact, in Latin, with a detainee imprisoned on a charge of demagogic activity! Rosenkranz made his report in 1844. All the other witnesses were doubtless still alive. No possible doubt.

Next the interpretation: Was not the one suggested by Rosenkranz tailored to the circumstances? After all, his *Hegels Leben* was published under watchful eyes.

The reading of Hegel's deed may vary.

A poet may savour the charm of this adventure, its romanticism, its sentimentality, its light irony. Enough to compose some verses: "On the Water".

But von Schuckmann's police were not poets. If they had observed the scene, how would they have understood it?

They had arrested the detainee because of his *political associations* with other "demagogues". Now here a group of suspect individuals use the cover of night to elude the surveillance of the sentinels and establish contact with the prisoner. An illegal and deliberate political act! They are in for it!

Amongst them — surprise! — Professor Hegel. Here is a fellow caught in compromising circumstances. Most of the victims of repression, as we have seen, had not done as much!

Never would our hypothetical investigators have allowed Rosenkranz's version. Did Hegel sense the "strangeness of the situation" only during the course of the expedition? Come on! In Rosenkranz's account everything points to premeditation. Hegel, a specialist in reflection, had the time to think: how could he have failed to understand that embarking under such conditions was compromising?

Besides, would his students have approached him, if they had not known his political leanings?

Rosenkranz speaks of the "innocence" of the detainee and, at the same time, tries to present Hegel as a "converter of demagogues" (*Demagogenbekehrer*). Two incompatible theses and both false.

Had the detainee not been *in fact* a "demagogue", the need to "convert" him would not have arisen.

But Rosenkranz on the other hand clearly shows that Hegel did not visit him with this intention, that he did not try to worm his way into his company in the role of an ideological agent of the government. Gaolers usually grant "sheep", who would destroy morale, easy access to political prisoners.

If Hegel was intending to serve the ends of the police, why choose to use Latin, incomprehensible to stool pigeons and sentinels? Would a "respectful official" (in Lucien Herr's words) or a "converter of demagogues" (as Rosenkranz depicts him) have had to fear a sentinel's gunshot? Missionaries of submission on occasion disguise themselves as friends of rebels to win their confidence. But they proceed without risk and without fear, whereas Hegel proceeded quietly on the water, in the dark, all lights extinguished and in silence, his heart pounding.

This fright of Hegel, at the moment of action, demonstrates the sincerity of his enterprise. Together with his students he had decided to make a gesture of solidarity. Did this gesture help the detainee? That is doubtful. But it clearly established a sense of complicity with those who carried it out; it gave them courage, and consolidated the convictions that had inspired it.

·········

We should not exaggerate the significance of this incident, but it does reveal a certain boldness on Hegel's part, verging on rashness. Although following the beaten track by day, when he cannot avoid it, he is a man who, by night, allows himself some strange liberties.

In any event it should not be thought that Hegel was unclear in what he was doing. He had nothing about him of the innocent who can be manipulated by a trick to do more than he desired. He knew how to use the tiller.

He recognized traps and dangers. He did not thoughtlessly expose himself to risks. He accepted them, when he so decided. He was experienced.

During his youth, a tyrannous régime had taught him how to dissimulate. Early on he took part in clandestine activities.

Recall the circumstances in which the "seminarians" of the *Stift* in Tübingen[4] lived at the time of the French Revolution. They organised in secret a revolutionary political club where Hegel showed himself to be the most impassioned orator. French newspapers were clandestinely circulated. It was forbidden to receive them, to hand them on, or to read them; yet the residents of the *Stift* discussed their contents with one another.

Hölderlin, Schelling and Hegel took part in planting a freedom tree — though this became known only later.* The club of young theologues aided the flight to France of a particularly compromised comrade, and took under their wing soldiers of the Republic imprisoned by the Allies, sometimes organizing their escape. Schelling was once accused of having made contact with the armies of the Revolution — in time of war![5]

Hegel lost his political innocence quite early.

At Bern and Frankfurt he wrote essays in a quite heterodox spirit — unpublishable texts that in fact remained unknown until 1907.

He composed political tracts which, his friends advised, should be kept to himself. If he did not offer to the public any of the works written during this period, it was not because he judged them inadequate; rather there were "external" reasons to justify his discretion: fear of censorship, of the courts, of hostile public opinion, and so on.

One significant fact: Hegel's first publication was the *Letters* of J.-J. Cart, a revolutionary work that he translated into German and annotated, while remaining anonymous.* Did the Berlin authorities know that Hegel, in the past, had spent time on such tasks?

* * * * * * * * *

Throughout his life, Hegel took precautions. The discrepancy between his published opinions and his letters, as well as between his "openable" letters and his "closed" letters continued unchanged.

He knew the police methods of his day. He was not unaware that they opened nearly all the correspondence entrusted to the post, and that they even dared on occasion to send suspects letters composed in their headquarters to lead them into self-betrayal. This is the way they had proceeded in the case of Knigge — and with success.[6]

As a result, whenever Hegel wanted to express himself somewhat more freely, he used what his friend, Niethammer, called "closed and private" mail, that is to say the good services of travelling friends who delivered the missives by hand.

As well, when he replied circumspectly to correspondents still unidentified, he slipped into his letters expressions that could "clear" him. Thus in his first answer to Duboc, whom he did not yet know, he pointed out in passing and without apparent necessity, that by his *Philosophy of Right* he had "greatly offended the demagogic populace."[7]

But what should we infer from this parenthetical clause? Should we take it literally? At the very same time, Hegel was in written contact with Ulrich, one of the most relentless and violent demagogues. And under what conditions?

The singular characteristics of Hegel's correspondence with Ulrich are revealed to us by the only document that survives: a letter from Ulrich to Hegel, dated August 2, 1822. It contains nothing reprehensible, and it is doubtless for this reason that, by exception, Hegel did not destroy it. But it sheds light on the tactics of the two correspondents.

Ulrich gives the following instructions:

> If it pleases you to answer, which would give me great pleasure, would you be so kind as to address the letter, which I will shred as usual after having read it closely, to Mr. Eckhardt in Wittmoldt, near Plön-en-Holstein.[8]

Hegel corresponded, therefore, with an exile, at a time when he was being sought by the Prussian police. But all the letters from Hegel to Ulrich, as well as those from Ulrich to

Hegel were destroyed upon reception. As an additional precaution, Hegel did not address his letters to Ulrich directly, but through an intermediary.

In addition, everything leads us to think that neither Hegel nor Ulrich in these conditions would have been so foolish as to entrust to the "public and open" post a letter addressed from Plön (an emminently suspect residence) to Professor Hegel, or from Berlin to Plön. Once again, travellers must have served as postmen.

Did Hegel correspond secretly with others in the same way? It is now impossible to reach a definite conclusion on this point.

But as far as correspondence was concerned, Hegel's fears always loomed very large. We find an amusing reflection of this in a letter from Hegel to his wife, during a trip to Austria.

He was afraid that Mrs. Hegel would express herself too freely. He cautioned "that the letters are read in Austrian territory and thus are not to contain anything political."

But at the same time he realized that this warning was itself dangerous, because it could lead to a suspicion that Mrs. Hegel had reprehensible political ideas and an inclination to express them. His own letter risked inspection by the authorities as well, and not only in Austria. He knew this well. Consequently, he surrounded his remark by diversionary phrases:

> It is unnecessary to caution you ... which in any case would not happen, coming from you.[9]

Such were Hegel's methods and subterfuges. Only with caution should commentators use certain conformist statements in his "openable" letters. The addressees who knew the author read between the lines. They smiled at the passages Hegel dedicated to the police on duty. Do not be more naive than they!

2. The Calculated Risk

Dangerous associates, assistance to the persecuted, indiscreet interventions, a secret collection, clandestine correspondence, a nocturnal expedition; did Hegel really take account of the risks he ran?

Imagine the boat challenged on the Spree, Ulrich's letter on the desk of von Kamptz, or the collection for de Wette discovered and seized. How could this "official, intimate with law and order, realistic and subservient" have answered the questions of the police?

And how would the police have taken his answers, surely adroit, but doubtless not very convincing? Would not this "generous" philosopher, friend of the "innocent" and enemy of "juvenile disorder" have made, in his turn, the acquaintance of an essential and deeply-rooted feature of "this rich internal articulation of the moral world that is the State": prison?

One could strictly allow that he intervened in favour of the accused; one could be persuaded that he believed in their "innocence," or at least defended them "from the outside," without supporting them "from the inside." Yet in the long run this interpretation of Hegel's attitude must lose all plausibility.

The evidence of conduct that was no longer simply equivocal, but unquestionably contrary to the laws and regulations would have to remove all doubts.

Hegel's policy seems to have been one of calculated risk: go as far as possible, but stop short of the breaking point. In fact he often came within a hair's breadth of the critical limit. At times he boldly moved forward, almost touching it.

Moreover, his friends and protegés, for their part, had no scruples about compromising him, at times needlessly. Did they have to boast of his friendship in front of the investigators, by mentioning him among the most dangerous suspects?[10]

The police investigated practically all of Asverus's friends and acquaintances. Was Hegel the only one they overlooked?

The latter was not aware of all that they knew about him. In 1820, he sojourned at Dresden. In Förster's company he visited the battlefields in the region, where his friend had distinguished himself a short while before. Did he suspect that he was observed in his association with this man? A police report later mentions him, with respect to a *Burschenschaft* convention at Dresden:

> Hegel from Berlin, doctor and professor, lived at *The Blue Star*, from August 27 to September 11, 1820. He arrived in the company of the

Prussian Lieutenant Förster and together they visited the surrounding area.

The same report mentions the presence of Bernhard von Yxküll, another friend of Hegel,[11] and another suspect.

Hegel was aware of the dangers and the threats, without always grasping them in their imminent detail. That was enough. He knew that he was condemned to live in a dangerous environment. As early as 1819, after touching on the de Wette affair, the new censorship measures, and Asverus's remand to the criminal court, he wrote:

> You surely understand as well, moreover, that all this does not help brighten one's spirits. I am about to be fifty years old, and I have spent thirty of these fifty years in these ever-unrestful times of hope and fear. I had hoped that for once we might be done with it. Now I must confess that things continue as ever. Indeed, in one's darker hours it seems they are getting ever worse.[12]

The date shows that Hegel was not yet at the end of his troubles!

He soon complained to Niethammer of the fact that the professor of philosophy is exposed, by vocation, to suspicions and dangers, and on this occasion vented his spleen against the demagogues: he acknowledged the final justice of the authorities' attitude![13] But this was an "openable" letter, dated 1821. Hegel continued, after this, to aid the persecuted.

In the same letter, Hegel brought up other worries. The theories of his friend Oken, the naturalist who had been accused of atheism, had just been banned in Berlin. And he added:

> You know that, on the one hand, I am an anxious man, and, on the other hand, that I like tranquility. It is not exactly a comfort to see a storm rise up each year, even if I can be persuaded that at the most only a few drops of a light rain will touch me. But you also know that being at the middle point also has the advantage of affording more accurate knowledge of what is *likely*, so that one can be more assured of one's interest and situation.[14]

Hegel would get used to seeing many more storms arise after 1821.

But why was he afraid of being "touched by only a few drops"? What was the real value of the protection he benefited from in high places?

We may think that until Hardenberg's death in 1822 he did not risk much, provided he still observed certain rules of prudence. But these he neglected when he took the boat into the vicinity of the bailiff's prison.

And then, after 1822, as the government's political stance became more reactionary, whose support could he count on? That of Schultze, himself suspect? That of Altenstein, to be sure, but this minister was not invulnerable.

Hegel could hardly rely on anything but his own merits, challenged by the feudal class, and on a certain influence of public opinion. As Niethammer wrote in 1822, the reactionaries had given themselves a dangerous alternative. They would either have to rid the University of its best teachers or else show themselves to be "evil pursuers of plots",[15] or, as we say today, miserable "witchhunters".

With the help of luck, Hegel held his own. His fate depended on one admission more or one less at Cousin's trial, the failure to arrest a witness, the discretion of a friend, the efforts of Altenstein, and his own diplomacy, which on occasion succeeded in making von Kamptz play his game.

But he needed it, often enough. The equilibrium constantly threatened to shatter. Hegel walked a tightrope.

NOTES

1. "Hegel," *Grande Encyclopédie*, 998.

2. That is, one of his students.

3. *Hegels Leben*, 338.

4. The well-known Protestant theological seminary. Hegel had been a resident there for several years, along with Hölderlin and Schelling.

5. See K. Klüpfel, *Geschichte und Beschreibung der Universität Tübingen* (Tübingen, 1849) 267-269.

6. See A Fournier, *Historische Studien und Skizzen*, (Prag/Leipzig, 1885) III, 17.

7. *Briefe*, II, 329; *Letters*, 493.

8. *Briefe*, II, 331-332. Lacking this single letter, we would have no knowledge that any contact between Hegel and Ulrich had existed.

9. *Briefe* III, 48-9; *Letters*, 610.

10. See Asverus, cited by Hoffmeister, *Briefe*, II, 436.

11. See *Briefe*, II, Hoffmeister's note, 482.

12. *Briefe*, II, 219; *Letters*, 451.

13. *Briefe*, II, 271; *Letters*, 470.

14. *Briefe*, II, 271-2; *Letters*, 470.

15. *Briefe*, II, 336.

Part Three

The Judgement of
Marx and Engels

A careful examination of documents can dissolve prejudices. However, some historians never get to the point of forgetting outdated clichés; and, in the hope of reviving them, they use the argument from authority: they appeal to Marx and Engels – two revolutionaries who know how to categorize people politically. These are masters of their subject; no one better than they to assess Hegel; so we should pay attention to their counsel.

We certainly do not want to challenge the value of their evidence. But before accepting it, we need to recall its terms, its exact sense, and its purpose.

Do not forget that Marx and Engels had only fragmentary documentation at their disposal. They knew scarcely anything of the details concerning Hegel we have just cited.

They knew nothing about his revolutionary youth: the *Club* of Tübingen, or the *Letters* of J-J Cart. They could not even suspect the whole range of manuscripts, nonconformist both politically and religiously, which Nohl published only in 1907.

Incomplete as it was, the edition of Hegel's *Letters* which his son published contained virtually nothing of the affairs of Asverus, Carové, Ulrich, Henning, Förster, or even Cousin. Nevertheless, with regard to Hegel's hostility to the restoration it provided evidence which one would search in vain for in his works.

But it appeared only in 1887. Marx had been dead for two years. Did Engels, 67 years old at the time and burdened with many responsibilities, take the time to consult it?

One thing is certain: ever since the death of Marx as well as that of Engels, every new discovery has served to accentuate the progressive features of the Berlin philosopher's concrete personality.

All the same, despite the inadequacy of their information, the Hegel whom they evaluated principally on the basis of his published work was considered to be neither reactionary nor even conservative.

This was especially so during their youth, in the period when they had adopted a political stance that was nothing more than democratic.

Later on, once they had adopted the communist position, they attacked Hegel's belated disciples. At that time they were particularly concerned about a sort of Hegelian *school*; and they regretted seeing how some of their friends had become fixed in an attitude that had been rendered out of date by events.

I

The Young Engels

Let us go back to the articles and essays written by Friedrich Engels between 1839 and 1842. In those days our author belonged to the political movement that had derived from the *Burschenschaft*. In 1840 he said to his sister:

Listen, for Christmas make me a new cigar case in black, red and gold, those are the only colours I like.[1]

These symbolic — and subversive — colours were those of the Lützow Hunting Corps, the colours of Körner and Förster, and of the *Burschenschaft* as well. Much later the German republic would use them for its flag.

As a bourgeois democrat, the young Engels proved to be particularly active and resolute. Auguste Cornu attests to the "revolutionary enthusiasm" that inspired all the works of this period.[2]

Without a doubt Engels was converted to Hegelianism at the same time as his liberal and revolutionary tendencies were becoming more radical.[3] As he gradually distanced himself from the pietism of his youth, he became at once both more Hegelian and more democratic.

In 1840 this young revolutionary liberal — and by no means the most insignificant nor the least courageous — regarded Hegel as the authoritative spokesman for a doctrine that was vital and still practical. The passing of ten years had not weakened the force of those theories.

Engels did not miss any opportunity of declaring his commitment to Hegelianism. In 1839, while criticizing an opponent of Hegel, he vigorously asserted:

> And despite Leo, the [Hegelian] school is spreading from day to day.
> ... *A propos*, Leo is the only academic teacher in Germany who
> zealously defends the hereditary aristocracy.[4]

He even composed a dramatic poem in which Leo and the
Hegelians confronted each other: Hegel's opponent was made
to appear ridiculous.[5] He admired the left-wing Hegelian,
Bruno Bauer, who on public occasions never ceased protesting
that the Hegelian theory of the state "far surpassed in its
liberalism and decisiveness the attitudes current in southern
Germany."[6]

Engels vigorously supported the Hegelian party when
Schelling arrived in Berlin to attack it. Against Schelling's
criticisms he used the style of Förster's eulogy at Hegel's
funeral to state in 1842:

> It will be *our* business to follow the source of his thinking and to
> shield the great man's grave from abuse. We are not afraid to fight.
> Nothing more desirable could have happened to us than for a time to
> be *ecclesia pressa*.[7]

"We"—that is to say, the disciples of this Hegel whom
Engels the revolutionary had chosen as master. "His philosophy
of history," he said, "is anyway written as from my own heart."[8]
For him Hegel stood as a symbol confronting the scribes of
reaction.[9]

In an important article of 1841, on Ernst Moritz Arndt, he
tried to situate Hegel historically. He wrote:

> Even before this latest world-shaking event [the revolutions of 1830]
> two men had been working quietly on the development of the
> German, or as it is preferably called, the modern spirit.

These two men were Börne* and Hegel, whose theories
Engels wanted to unite.

After having put in place the approach of the former, and
even though he was considering only the public expression of
Hegel's thought, which, as we have seen, lags far behind the
concrete behaviour of the philosopher, he described the role of
the latter this way:

Authority did not take the trouble to work its way through the abstruse forms of Hegel's system and his brazen style; but then, how could it have known that this philosophy would venture from the quiet haven of theory into the stormy sea of actuality, that it was already brandishing its sword in order to strike directly against existing practice? For Hegel himself was such a solid, orthodox man, whose polemic was directed at precisely those trends which the state's power rejected,[10] at rationalism and cosmopolitan liberalism! But the gentlemen at the helm did not appreciate that these trends were only combatted in order to make room for a higher, that the new teaching must find root itself in recognition of the nation before it could freely develop its living consequences.

Unaware of Hegel's secret activities, Engels then raised the question of the specific relations the philosopher had with the state. He first tried to define them, not without some hesitation; then in the end he gave up—it was not what was of interest:

> When Börne attacked Hegel he was perfectly right from his standpoint, but when authority protected Hegel, when it elevated his teaching almost to a Prussian philosophy of state, it laid itself open to attack, a fact which it now evidently regrets. Or did Altenstein, whose more advanced standpoint was a legacy of a more liberal age, receive such a free hand here that everything was laid to his account? Be that as it may....

Today Engels's second hypothesis has emerged victorious. We can credit "everything" to the account of Altenstein and his friends. The "authorities" did not protect Hegel. Stated simply: one of the men in power supported him ... As to the Prussian officials overall—the king, the court, and the ministers—they either opposed Hegel or were suspicious of him.
Engels added:

> Be that as it may, when after Hegel's death the fresh air of life breathed upon his doctrine, the "Prussian philosophy of the state" sprouted shoots of which no martyr had ever dreamt. Strauss will remain epoch-making in the theological field, Gans and Ruge in the political. Only now do the faint nebulae of speculation resolve themselves into the shining stars of the ideas which are to light the movement of the century. One may accuse Ruge's aesthetic criticism of being prosaic and petrified within the schematism of doctrine; yet

credit must go to him for showing the political side of the Hegelian
system to be in accord with the spirit of the times and for restoring it
in the nation's esteem. Gans has done this only indirectly, by
carrying the philosophy of history forward into the present; Ruge
openly expressed the liberalism of Hegelianism, and Köppen
supported him; neither was afraid of incurring enmity, both pursuing
their course, even at the risk of a split in the school, and all due
respect to their courage for it!

In this way Engels shows how the Hegelian school sprang to
life after Hegel's death. He could recall that Ruge had become
a Hegelian during his detention in prison, while Hegel was still
teaching; and that Gans had begun to develop the practical
implications of Hegelianism well before 1831, dying himself
only a few years after Hegel, in 1839. Had Gans really "carried
Hegel's philosophy of history forward into the present"?
Insaying that, Engels might simply have been following a
mistaken tradition, current for some time among Hegelian
circles, according to which Hegel was not the author of the final
lecture of the *Philosophy of History*. The manuscripts now
extant entirely disprove this tradition. The merit which Engels
here accorded to Gans reverts to Hegel himself.

Engels was interested more in reconstructing the history of
the Hegelian school than in recovering the concrete political
attitude of Hegel. He did not know about the hidden life of the
philosopher; he took account only of his published works and
the lectures inadequately edited by disciples, who twisted them
in a suggestive way; he based his reading on uncertain
biographical and historical information.

Nonetheless, despite all these reasons for discounting his
claims, Hegelianism seemed, from the liberal perspective which
he adopted in 1841, to be the theoretical foundation for the
progressive political movement of his day. He wrote:

The enthusiastic, unshakable confidence in the idea, inherent in the
New Hegelianism, is the sole fortress in which the liberals can find
safe retreat whenever reaction gains a temporary advantage over
them with aid from above.

and he noted that

Hegel's practical importance for the present (not his philosophical significance for eternity) is not to be judged by the pure theory of the system.[11]

Engel's views of the political tendencies of Hegel's doctrine did not fundamentally change when he became communist. In 1851-52 he published under Marx's name a study that was attributed to the latter until quite recently: *Revolution and Counter-revolution in Germany*. The two friends worked in strict collaboration and took little care to distinguish their respective efforts. Marx evidently agreed with the content of this study.

When reviewing the history of German political developments, the author situated Hegel in the following way:

Lastly, German philosophy, that most complicated, but at the same time most sure thermometer of the development of the German mind, had declared for the middle class, when Hegel pronounced, in his *Philosophy of Law*, Constitutional Monarchy to be the final and most perfect form of Government. In other words, he proclaimed the approaching advent of the middle classes of the country to political power.[12]

In 1820 the Prussian opposition dreamed neither of a republic, nor of socialism, nor of communism. They wanted to establish a constitutional monarchy, which would require a considerable evolution in the political order, or even a revolution, such as occurred in 1848. In this country where absolutism reigned supreme, a work that *announced* a new political regime and which anticipated such a change of course certainly did not work in favour of the *status quo*, nor for a return to feudalism.

Hegel had entertained the ideals of the middle class of his day. At the time this was the only revolutionary social class in Prussia, as compared to the reactionary aristocracy and the conservative petty bourgeoisie.

Indeed in 1847, when the proletariat began to participate in the political life, Engels stressed this point:

In Germany the bourgeoisie is not only not in power; it is even the most dangerous enemy of the existing governments.[13]

The *Communist Manifesto* of 1848 took serious account of this situation. There Marx and Engels announced in their turn "the imminent arrival of the country's bourgeoisie to political power!" They wrote:

> The Communists turn their attention chiefly to Germany because that country is on the eve of a bourgeois revolution that is bound to be carried out under more advanced conditions of European civilization, and with a much more developed proletariat, than that of England in the seventeenth, and of France in the eighteenth century, and because the bourgeois revolution will be but the prelude to an immediately following proletarian revolution.[14]

In 1848, the constitutional monarchy whose theory Hegel had developed in 1820 was still central to the programme of the German revolutionary middle class.

NOTES

1. Marx-Engels, *Collected Works*, II (1975) 518.

2. A. Cornu, *K.Marx et F. Engels* (Paris, 1955) I, 255.

3. A. Cornu, *op.cit.*, 217.

4. Marx-Engels, *Collected Works*, II (1975) 452.

5. Ibid. 435-7.

6. Cf. Cornu, *op.cit.*, 265n1.

7. In the essay "Schelling on Hegel," (1841) in Marx-Engels, *Collected Works*, II, (1975) 187.

8. Engels to Wilhelm Gräber, Marx-Engels, *Collected Works*, II (1975), 481.

9. "Retrograde signs of the times", Ibid. 47-48.

10. Allusion to Hegel's attack on Fries.

11. All citations are taken from the article on Ernst Moritz Arndt, in Marx-Engels, *Collected Works*, II (1975) 142-144.

12. "Revolution and Counter-revolution in Germany," in Marx-Engels, *Collected Works*, XI, (1978) 14.

13. "The Constitutional Question in Germany," Marx-Engels, *Collected Works*, VI (1975) 76.

14. "Manifesto of the Communist Party," Marx-Engels, *Collected Works*, VI (1975) 519.

II

The Critique of Hegel's Philosophy of Right

Between 1820 and 1848 the German proletariat arrived on stage and began to push the middle class into the wings. The bourgeoisie did not yet enjoy power, and already it found itself in danger of losing it. Before even having had a chance of existing, the German bourgeois state was threatened with collapse. The grave digger knocked at the door of the delivery room.

About 1844 Marx and Engels laid the foundation for their new conception of the world, history, social life and politics. In doing that, they had to break with the past – with even the most developed doctrines yet achieved; in a way the *Critique of Hegel's Philosophy of Right*, which Marx composed at this time, marks one stage in this breach.[1]

Inevitably Marx had to settle his account with the Hegelian philosophy of law, to criticize middle class thought in its most distinguished form, if he wanted to elaborate a new theory.

After this critique, Hegel's doctrine had become conservative in comparison with a revolutionary program which now surpassed it; but it did not cease to be progressive when compared with a political reality which it wanted to replace. Although it continued to be in advance with respect to the institutions of 1820, it no longer retained first place in the range of doctrines.

When Marx vigorously exorcised the witchcraft of the *Philosophy of Right*, he had two ends principally in view.

The first was to convince himself and his friends that the Hegelian doctrine was false; it did not correctly represent objective reality. Rich and interesting though it be – superior as well to all its contemporaries – it could nevertheless no longer succeed in satisfying the requirements of scientific thought. Marx affirmed this, and endeavoured to go beyond it. From then on it ceased to express the most advanced thinking. Despite several fragmentary indications, for example, it did not contribute to the socialist movement that had just been born. Even less did it anticipate the economic, social and political theory that Marx was beginning to articulate.

For this reason Marx, with great polemical vigour, condemned the contradictions, the faulty inferences, the mysticism, the idealist masquerade of reality, and the critical weaknesses that marked Hegelianism.

Marx's second purpose was to show how this theory, appropriate for the middle class, not only in 1820, but also in 1844, was now applying the brakes to the progress of the young intellectuals who were bound too much to its letter, preventing them from rallying to the camp of the proletariat. In fact, a good many "young Hegelians" were dogmatically inclined to certain anachronistic formulas of Hegel. Such an idolatry fixed them into an outdated attitude, and held them back from adopting the behaviour required by the new conditions of German political life.

From 1820 on, the middle class had enjoyed a rapid advance. Its demands had taken a more radical turn. The appearance of the proletariat as a political force made some social transformations all the more urgent.

The systematic critique of the Hegelian doctrine of the state assumed decisive political importance. It had to be conducted rigorously, with no quarter and with scientific intransigence. Marxism could arise only on the ruins of bourgeois ideology.

So Marx undertook a refutation of the *Philosophy of Right*; although not yet fully Marxist, it uncovered the Hegelian "mystifications", and, as J. Hyppolite has shown, identified the quite concrete problems, not only of German political life, but also of our own time.[2] Having done this, according to E. Bottigelli, Marx

> introduced a new method. ... He stressed the contradictory character of the bourgeois state; that represented a step further towards a revolutionary conception. ... The break with the bourgeoisie would be decisive.[3]

The fruit of this effort—some notes, a draft—Marx refused to have published, for, thanks to what he was writing, his thought was continuing to move on; at the end it no longer recognized itself in the traces left by its movement. So the *Critique of the Philosophy of Right* does not offer us a completed theory, but rather the sketch of a transition.

In it Marx does not raise the question of whether Hegel *in his own times* was progressive or conservative. He was much more occupied with discovering the real relations between Hegelian theory and political reality, the better to appreciate its theoretical value and its *current* revolutionary effectiveness.

In fact, everything wears out. In a new setting a political theory can easily lose every progressive import that, despite its weaknesses, it retained at the time of its publication. Marx criticized the scientific value and the political tendencies of Hegel's ideas; but he took the same approach to those of Rousseau, the Jacobins of 1793, and the Saint Simonians of 1830—without denying in the least, for all that, their progressive or revolutionary effectiveness *in their own times* and in certain concrete circumstances.

After all, Marx's comments could apply just as easily to chapters in *The Social Contract* as to the paragraphs in the *Philosophy of Right*, to which he actually referred. For in his eyes it is the bourgeois state that is contradictory, not just the way Hegel presented it.

To be sure, Marx did not let slip the opportunity of noting, in Hegel's work, the aspects that were conservative even in the context of their own time. Over all, the orientation of the *Philosophy of Right*, by heralding "the near future of the bourgeoisie," is progressive—certainly so in 1820. But we should not be deceived by the appearance of systematic unity that Hegel wanted to give his *Principles*. Some of them sit uneasily with others. Hegel is neither a more coherent nor a more rigorous thinker than his great predecessors. His main political thesis is soiled by impurities. In addition, the practical constraints on publishing the work required of him prudence and conformity.

Thus, for example, when reading Paragraph 310, in which Hegel develops the conditions which the candidates for the representative assembly ought to fulfil, Marx exclaims:

> Here the thoughtless inconsistency and the *'administrative'* sense of Hegel become truly *repulsive*. ... All that is missing is for Hegel to demand that the *estates* should pass an *examination* set by their worshipful government. Hegel here descends almost to servility. We see him infected through and through with the miserable arrogance of the *Prussian* civil service which in its bureaucratic stupidity grandly looks down on the 'self-confidence' of the 'people's own subjective opinion.' For Hegel, the 'state' is everywhere here identical with the 'government.'[4]

But notice that these pejorative phrases do not express the sentiment of the whole critique Marx makes of the *Philosophy of Right*. They refer to *one paragraph*. It is *here* that the Hegelian inconsistency ends by reaching *almost* to servility. The reproach stands alone. We should recall in addition that he is considering Hegel's submission to a government which, in his day, could scarcely be compared with that to which Marx was subject in 1844. It was that of the "half-reformer" Hardenberg, helped by the "liberal" Altenstein, heir of Stein and Schön. And let us recall Marx's comment , with respect to the Prussian constitution:

> Stein, Hardenberg and Schön had one opinion and Rochow, Arnim and Eichhorn another.[5]

Marx did not take on the task of dogmatically passing judgement on Hegel. For him it was not a question of stigmatizing the diverse faults of the Berlin philosopher. He himself indicated that,

> No suspicion is cast upon the particular conscience of the philosopher, but his essential form of consciousness is construed, raised to a definite shape and meaning, and in this way also transcended.[6]

From this perspective Marx wanted above all to expose the contradictions contained in the Hegelian theory of law, into which the real contradictions of the modern state had been transposed. He translated Hegel into a more comprehensible language, then showed the relation between that thought and empirical reality; he disclosed the mystification contained in the supposed "deduction" of political categories, and concluded with the need to *invert* from then on the Hegelian method. In particular he was led to reject the making of "civil society" dependent on the state, as Hegel had proposed, and to show on the contrary how the state rested on civil society.[7]

In 1859 Marx defined the import of the work he had begun in 1844:

> The first work which I undertook for a solution of the doubts which assailed me was a critical review of the Hegelian philosophy of right. ... My investigation led on to the result that legal relations as well as forms of state are to be grasped neither from themselves nor from the so-called general development of the human mind, but rather have their roots in the material conditions of life, the sum total of which Hegel, following the example of the Englishmen and Frenchmen of the eighteenth century, combines under the name of 'civil society.'[8]

In his *Critique of the Philosophy of Right* Marx chose to attack Hegel precisely because he described the modern state—which did not yet exist in Prussia. Even if he had not intended anything else than a derivative political analysis, how could he picture Hegel as a "reactionary" in such circumstances?

In reality Marx was aiming further afield. He was taking issue with a general conception of the state and of social life. In the manner of Rousseau and the Jacobins, Hegel had thought it possible to deduce the state as an essential reality, and he conferred on the results of his deduction an absolute and eternal character. As a result he presented the contradictory essence of the bourgeois state as if it were the eternal essence of any state.[9]

Such a mystification did not bother the Prussian middle class any more than it had stopped the revolutionaries of 1789 in their outburst. The bourgeois revolutionary takes pride in thinking that he is working for eternity.

But the proletarian revolutionary does not let himself be deceived by this illusion; he does not bow down before this trumped up eternity. Even before the bourgeois state had been established in Prussia, Marx discerned in its principles the seeds of its inevitable demise.

Hegel did not clearly perceive the deeply rooted contradictions inherent in the modern state he was describing.10 He was content to anticipate their existence. He announced the imminent rise of the bourgeoisie, but did not foresee its ultimate fall. He discerned nothing beyond the next historical stage. This partial blindness betrayed a failure in applying his method, which calls for the universal decay of institutions. It led to methodological inconsistency.[11]

The constitutional monarchy which Hegel seemed to offer as the definitive political regime would perish like its predecessors. Its contradictions would destroy it. It requires a more democratic regime, even if it remains middle class. Even in 1842 Marx intended to make that clear. At that time he confided to Ruge his plan for

> a criticism of Hegelian natural law, insofar as it concerns the *internal political system*. The central point is the struggle against *constitutional monarchy* as a hybrid which from beginning to end contradicts and abolishes (*aufheben*) itself.[12]

Such characteristics are evidently found in all political regimes. Each of them suffers from an internal contradiction that will cause it to perish. That in no way prevents it from constituting an historical stage, higher than the one preceding.

The constitutional *monarchy* is no exception. It had its merits, and it maintained them for a long time – indeed even in 1830, in France. In a passage of the *Critique*, Marx notes: "The French constitution is an advance."[13] That referred to the constitutional regime introduced in France after the revolution of 1830. Would not constitutional monarchy have been acclaimed as an even more progressive requirement in the semi-feudal Prussia of 1820?

Marx was thinking of future revolutions. To understand their birth one had to succeed in analysing social reality and its internal contradictions more profoundly. If Hegel had not been able to do it himself, it was because of the "inadequacy of his principle"[14], and not because of a simple tactical accommodation.

In the *Critique of the Philosophy of Right* Marx was preparing to take over from Hegel. Methodologically he had benefited from the Hegelian initiative in some of its aspects. Substantively, he was preparing a break with idealism.

He sketched out the limits of the Hegelian state, and he condemned the "mysticism" and "mystification" of a theory that wanted to make it appear unlimited. He knew well enough that, in contrast with its contemporaries—with the theories of Haller, Ancillon, Savigny, and Fries, or with the feudal ideology—Hegel's theory scaled the heights of bourgeois thought, and provided it with its most serious, most reflective and most soundly based expression. He would not have directed his attack against it had he taken it to be regressive and already refuted.

On the contrary, by vanquishing Hegel, he saved himself the bother of combatting those who were already passé; and he captured the lead from his imitators. He reproached Max Stirner, who thought himself "advanced", for knowing the bourgeois liberalism "only in the sublimated form given it by Hegel and the school masters who depend on him."[15] In 1845 Stirner was slowing things down. But in 1820 the "school masters" were learning to read, and the "sublimated bourgeoisified liberalism" was waxing towards its Prussian hour.

NOTES

1. "Contribution to the Critique of Hegel's Philosophy of Law," in Marx-Engels, *Collected Works*, III (1975) 3-129. It was clearly a question of a *relative* breach which took its place dialectically on the basis of historical continuity.

2. See J. Hyppolite, "Marx's Critique of the Hegelian Concept of the State," in *Studies on Marx and Hegel*, tr. J. O'Neill (New York: Basic, 1969) 106-125.

3. In K. Marx, *Manuscrits de 1844* (Paris, 1962) Translator's Preface.

4. "Critique," in Marx-Engels, *Collected Works*, III (1975) 124, 127.

5. "Marginal Notes to the Accusations of the Ministerial Rescript," in Marx-Engels, *Collected Works*, I (1975) 362.

6. Notes in doctoral dissertation, Marx-Engels, *Collected Works*, I (1975) 84-5.

7. "Critique," Marx-Engels, *Collected Works*, III, 6-8.

8. "Preface to *A Contribution to the Critique of Political Economy*," in K. Marx and F. Engels, *Selected Works in One Volume*, (London: Lawrence and Wishart, 1968) 182.

9. "Critique," Marx-Engels, *Collected Works*, III, 73.

10. "Critique," Marx-Engels, *Collected Works*, III, 84, 91.

11. "Critique," Marx-Engels, *Collected Works*, III, 91, 95.

12. Marx-Engels, *Collected Works*, I (1975) 382-3.

13. "Critique," Marx-Engels, *Collected Works*, III, 113.

14. "Notes to doctoral dissertation," Marx-Engels, *Collected Works*, I, 84.

15. "The German Ideology," Marx-Engels, *Collected Works*, V (1976) 197.

III

Hegel's Inheritance

Marx and Engels had a marked preference for drawing on the work of Hegel, the author they cited continuously and almost always in a flattering way. From time to time they renewed their efforts to locate themselves with respect to him.

Thus in 1886, in the first pages of his *Ludwig Feuerbach* and before tracing the fate of the Hegelian school, Engels assessed once more the thought of its founder.

He began by condemning the philosophical and political blindness, as well as the intellectual bankruptcy, of the majority of Hegel's contemporaries; neither the "narrow-minded government" nor the "equally narrow-minded liberals" grasped the revolutionary essence of Hegel's philosophy.[1]

It was thanks to their being so obtuse that Hegel could lead the life of a university professor, of an officially authorized educator of the young. Unaware of the anxiety, the threats, and the dangerous activities that in fact marked this existence, Engels contrasted its apparent calm to the definitely more disturbed and painful fate of the hunted, destitute and refractory revolutionary. Doubtless he was thinking of the contrast between the life of Marx and that of Hegel.

The Hegelian philosophy, he said, had been attacked "by those people who were then regarded as the representatives of the revolution." But this was because they misinterpreted the most central affirmations of the *Philosophy of Right*, in particular that which states:

All that is rational is real; and all that is real is rational.

Engels was right. It was indeed such assertions on the part of Hegel that had aroused the greatest animosity among the "narrow minded liberals" of his time. Engels reaffirmed the real, profoundly revolutionary, significance of these statements, following closely the indications that Hegel himself provided. Then he drew those implications of Hegel's philosophy that only Heine, more recently, had been able to see.[2]

He stressed "the true significance and the revolutionary character of the Hegelian philosophy" not only in what concerns the general problem of truth but also in what affects the explanation of historical development.[3] He noted that the Hegelian dialectic – as well as that of Marx – had necessarily a conservative moment: "It recognizes that definite stages of knowledge and society are justified for their time and circumstances." But overall "its revolutionary character is absolute." On this point Engels's only reproach was that Hegel had not stated all this with full precision.[4]

The Hegelian method admits of a legitimate conservative moment, which saved it from sinking into instability. Each political regime and each social structure that historical development installs on the ruins of its predecessor retains a temporary legitimacy, actuality and necessity. Engels did not reproach Hegel for this conservative moment in the dialectic, which in no way prevents it from becoming the revolutionary method *par excellence*.

Nonetheless, Hegel still introduced a conservatism alien to the method in attempting to construct a definitive system. In doing so he followed a conservative tendency in the usual sense of the term. Engels did not hide this. On the contrary, he insisted on it at great length; in his exposition we rediscover the ideas Marx had already propounded in his *Critique of the Philosophy of Right*.

If it is proper to credit to each political regime a relative validity during the time it responds positively to the historical conditions that gave it birth, it is illegitimate to ascribe to it eternal worth.

Yet this is what Hegel seems to do. He immortalizes one stage of the historical development arbitrarily – that of the bourgeois state whose imminent inauguration he announced. "Thus," says Engels, "the revolutionary side [of Hegel's theory] becomes smothered beneath the overgrowth of the conservative side."[5]

And this political conservatism prevents a radical application of the method to practical problems. Hegel anticipates a form of political development that would itself be final.

> And so we find [Engels observes] at the conclusion of the *Philosophy of Right* that the absolute idea is to be realized in that monarchy based on social estates which Frederick William III so persistently but vainly promised to his subjects, that is, in a limited, moderate, indirect rule of the possessing classes suited to the petty-bourgeois German condition of that time; and moreover the necessity of the nobility is demonstrated to us in a speculative fashion.

And Engels draws his conclusion:

> The inner necessities of the system are, therefore, of themselves sufficient to explain why a thoroughly revolutionary method of thinking produced an extremely tame political conclusion.[6]

The dialectical method did not allow a preview only of simple reforms, but also, and especially, of revolutions. It wiped away all hope of a definitive stability. Inspired by the fugue of the method, Engels regrets the relative moderation of the Hegelian political program.

He does not set Hegel's specific attitude against that of his contemporaries such as Fries or Haller, nor against the political situation of Prussia in 1820. He opposes the Hegel of the system to the Hegel of the method to show the brakes applied by the former on the latter. Nevertheless, although it does not maintain all the promises of the method, the system does not ridicule the hopes of its time.

Capable of powerful release, but bothered by obstacles, the athlete has not thrown the javelin very far. Yet he has at least grasped it, and its trajectory is indeed pointed towards the future.

The word "tame" by which Engels characterizes the political conclusion of Hegel does not refer to the political attitude represented in France by the "moderates". It translates the German term *zahm* (soft, docile, or tractable); Engels is thus remarking that Hegel, advocate of an explosive dialectic, does not achieve results as unsettling as one would have expected. The fetters of his age that Engels described had held him back.

Does he think Hegel could have gone further? Like Marx, he seems fascinated by an essential Hegelian contradiction: Hegel had shown himself sufficiently progressive to set forth the most detailed expression of middle class thought; but he went no further. He comprehended the bourgeois state; but he stayed there. And yet his method prohibits every stop and excludes every stasis.

In particular this paradox erupts in the *Philosophy of Right*. In no work of Hegel did the system forget the method so thoroughly. Hegel's example confirms what he had himself so often said: no thinker is in advance of his time.

In 1820 the constitutional monarchy retained the colours of the dawn, and the thinker of the dialectic did not predict that there would be a dusk for it as well. At least he did not make such a prediction explicit.

In his judgement, however, on the person of Hegel, who lived in a period of an exceptional equilibrium of political forces and in a Prussia where no coherent political parties existed, Engels showed a great deal of foresight.

We should not forget that in Engels's day Hegel was universally taken for a reactionary. No one, except indeed Engels himself, challenged this evaluation; those who did not hate Hegel despised him. Only much later would the Hegelian "renaissance" emerge. In this sphere as well, Engels swam against the current.

Against such a background Engels (who did not commit himself to writing a detailed biography and who at the time had to be content with publishing monographs) proceeds to rehabilitate Hegel—a scandalous act in the eyes of most of his contemporaries.

In a formula that is not stated dogmatically, he concedes that:

Hegel himself, despite the fairly frequent outbursts of revolutionary wrath in his works, seemed [*shien*] on the whole to be more inclined to the conservative side [*im ganzen mehr zur konservativen Seite zu neigen.*][7]

This judgement, expressly based on the works of Hegel as they were known at the time, is perhaps the only one where Engels allows himself to reach the point of "inclining on the whole more" towards the image of a conservative Hegel.

But he straightaway clarifies the sense by recalling once again the opposition between the system and the method, and Hegel's preference for system.

He is not thereby prevented from placing the *Philosophy of Right* among the numerous works of Hegel which were "epoch-making." How could a work thus characterize the historical period in which it appeared if it introduced nothing new, if it were satisfied with repeating its antecedents, if it did nothing more than advocate the retention of what was already known and achieved?

The tone of Engels's few pages leaves no doubt about the way he assessed Hegel: How could this "man of encyclopaedic erudition", this "creative genius", developer of "a wealth of thought which is astounding even today", — how could the philosopher with whom "philosophy comes to an end" and "who summed up its whole development in the most splendid fashion," even as he "showed us the way out of it" — how could the author of a system which produced "a tremendous effect" and whose "views penetrated the most diverse sciences" — how could such a man have been reactionary?

Does reaction ever create anything? Hegel himself reminds us: in most cases it only dreams of illicitly imprinting its seal on what others build.[8]

Marx and Engels could legitimately decipher the regressive features in "so powerful a work as Hegelian philosophy, which had exercised so enormous an influence on the intellectual development of the nation."[9] But neither the one nor the other had agreed with reducing all of it, including the political views, to the status of an episodic failure.

On the contrary they staked their reputation on reclaiming it. Despite his previous attacks on Hegel, Marx ventured in the Preface to the second edition of *Capital* to declare himself "the pupil of that mighty thinker."[10]

Some commentators succumb to personal prejudice in sharpening Marx and Engels's critique of Hegel. The latter often cite Hegel's merits without ever mentioning his weaknesses. With respect to Hegel's personal political opinions they show themselves to be quite circumspect in their judgements, and are in general content with citing common opinions on the subject to restrict their effect and attenuate their severity.

We offer one example of this moderation.

From time to time when speaking of Hegel Marx and Engels use the expression "philosopher of the state". However, they explicitly do not introduce this on their own initiative. They borrow the phrase from other writers, and cite it only to indicate the limits of its application.

Thus Engels could write: "When authority protected Hegel, when it elevated his teaching *almost* to a Prussian philosophy of the state, *it laid itself open to attack*, a fact which it now evidently regrets." (our italics) When he adds that "the 'Prussian philosophy of the state' sprouted shoots of which no party had ever dreamt," he takes care to place the expression in quotation marks. It does not fit and it makes him smile.[11]

For his part the young Marx stated:

> Hegel in his day believed that he had laid the basis for the Prussian constitution in his philosophy of law, and the government and the German public concurred in this belief. The way by which the government proved this was the official dissemination of his writings;[12] and the *public*, however, did so by accusing him of being the philosopher of the Prussian state, *as one can read in the old Leipzig conversational dictionary.* (our italics)[13]

The old conversational dictionary of Leipzig is to take full responsibility!

In *Ludwig Feuerbach*, Engels speaks of "the Hegelian system — raised in some degree [*gewissermassen*] to the rank of a royal Prussian philosophy of state!" But he immediately makes it clear that Hegel owed this promotion to the "narrow-minded governments" and "equally narrow-minded liberals" — to expose for our benefit a delicate irony.

In fact, it now appears that the "liberals" were even more "narrow-minded" than their governors: they stupidly allowed themselves to believe that the latter felt an inclination towards Hegelianism — which the facts prove false. It is evident, in any case, that Engels did not adopt their judgement. He undertook to show that if the government really "adopted" Hegel's philosophy, it was something that was not at all understood. As if to call on the ignorance and stupidity of the Prussian authorities for support!

Nor does he show himself soft on those of his socialist friends who let themselves adopt a strict and vulgar anti-Hegelianism.

Wilhelm Liebknecht, father of Karl Liebknecht, edited a socialist journal, the *Volksstaat*, in which Engels published some articles. Once Wilhelm had thought it proper to "complete" an allusion Engels had made to Hegel with a footnote.

Here is what Engels wrote to Marx about this incident:

> 'Monsieur' Wilhelm is no longer to be endured. ... Idiocies are now coming so frequently that it cannot be allowed any more. At the name, Hegel, the man added the comment: "To the public at large known as the discoverer (!) and glorifier (!!) of the royal Prussian *idea of the state*. (!!!) I have now served him appropriately in that regard and sent for him to publish as mild an explanation as possible in the circumstances.... This ignoramus has the insolence to want to be done with a chap like Hegel by means of the word 'Prussian' and thereby make the public believe *I* had said it. I have had enough of it.

And in the same severe tone Marx replied to Engels about their colleague, Wilhelm:

> I had written him that, if he only knows how to repeat the old Rotter-Welcker filth about Hegel, then he should better keep his mouth shut. He calls it: 'somewhat unceremoniously making short work of' Hegel, etc.; and when he adds inanities to Engels's article, then 'Engels can indeed (!) say it *in more detail*'. The man is really quite stupid."[14]

A hundred years after Marx and Engels' angry explosion one can still wish that this type of inanity about Hegel were no longer being repeated.

NOTES

1. "Ludwig Feuerbach and the End of Classical German Philosophy," in Marx-Engels, *Selected Works in One Volume*, (London, 1968) 596.

2. "Ludwig Feuerbach," *Selected Works*, 596.

3. Ibid. 598.

4. Ibid. 599.

5. "Ludwig Feuerbach," *Selected Works*, 599

6. Ibid. 599-600.

7. "Ludwig Feuerbach," *Selected Works*, 601.

8. See above, p. 32. *Briefe* II, 85-86; *Letters*, 325.

9. "Ludwig Feuerbach," *Selected Works*, 603.

10. *Capital*, Vol I, tr. Moore and Aveling, (London: Allen & Unwin, 1946) xxx. Recall that in 1844, *after* the *Critique of the Philosophy of Right*, Marx attempted to acquaint Proudhon with Hegelianism: "In the course of lengthy debates, often lasting all night, I infected him to his great injury with Hegelianism, which, owing to his lack of German, he could not study properly." Letter to J.B. von Schweitzer, in Marx-Engels, *Correspondence 1846-1895, A Selection*, (London: Lawrence & Wishart, 1936) 171.

11. "Ernst Moritz Arndt," in Marx-Engels, *Collected Works*, II, 143.

12. Marx appears to have been misinformed on this point.

13. "Marginal Notes to the Accusations of the Ministerial Rescript," in Marx-Engels, *Collected Works*, I, 362.

14. Engels to Marx, May 8, 1870; Marx to Engels, May 10, 1870; translated from Marx-Engels, *Werke* (Berlin, 1965) XXXII, 501, 503.

Conclusion

"Whoever knows me, will recognize me here." Hegel wrote these words under a sketch by Wilhelm Hensel: resolute face, drawn lips, the trace of a caustic smile.

What does it mean, to know Hegel?

To be sure, even if we knew nothing about his life, we could ascertain from his published works the essence of his prodigiously fertile thought. It is through the works that he has wielded such a wide, varied and decisive influence on posterity.

It is not without value, however, to unveil the philosopher as he really was. Knowing what Hegel did undeniably opens the way to an even better appreciation of what he said; it prompts us to give greater importance to some of his statements, moderating, or alternatively accentuating, their resonance, and adding nuances to traditional interpretations.

Such knowledge thus offers something of interest to the history of ideas, in which Hegelianism constitutes a notable moment. We cannot avoid examining the ties that bind so rich a thought to the concrete conditions in which it flourished.

If we have not succeeded in defining Hegel's political and social stance, or in characterizing his most prominent inclinations, we have at least set in relief quite significant actions, words, and associations, which were until now either unknown or known inaccurately.

Highlighting them serves to dispel the severest attacks from those who despise Hegel. In our day it cannot be maintained that Hegel was in his day a reactionary and a conformist. On the contrary, he thoroughly repudiated received ideas; he broke with established conventions; and he attacked prejudice and preconceptions. He felt neither nostalgia for the middle ages nor fear of modern times. He did not want to fix everything in its given form.

Yet we cannot classify him among the revolutionaries. He did not assume their style of life, even though from time to time he adopted their style of thinking. Perhaps he did not follow his ideas to their logical conclusion. We should remember that it was quite difficult to be a revolutionary in the Berlin of 1820, not only because of the danger involved, but also and especially because the situation was not revolutionary. The social and political life did not invite radical transformations, or rigorous and intransigent commitments.

In such conditions those who refused any compromise or believed in the possibility of an imminent political upheaval paid for their courageous choice with a quite noticeable lack of success. Do they really deserve the title: 'revolutionary'?

Reactionaries could scarcely be called the only ones who were 'monolithic' in Prussia between 1820 and 1830. Yet Hegel was not a man "of a single piece". Diverse and sometimes opposed tendencies divided his heart.

For us all kinds of difficulty can be found in this mixture. One has to evaluate, weigh, and measure out the diversity of component elements that one discerns when Hegel's works, behaviour and character are analyzed.

We have to consider both what he wrote and what he has been reported as having said. We have to gauge the depth of his silence.

What general orientation do we then discover? In what direction did Hegel advance in spite of all the hesitations, moments of regret and partial setbacks?

We believe we have established that, on the whole, his concrete political and social activity was that of a progressive. We would indeed characterize him a "reformist," if this term had not acquired a somewhat pejorative sense in the contemporary scene. Let us say: he was a progressive reformer.

He hoped that reforms would come about of necessity, not without a struggle to be sure, but without the eruption of violence. Nonetheless, the reforms he desired were inspired by the French Revolution. They were not insignificant and in fact required the revolution of 1848 to begin to receive an ephemeral realization.

Hegel was not satisfied with simply agreeing with political and intellectual progress. He advocated it, prepared its way, and worked on its behalf.

His achievement was profound and lasting; it has known a rich destiny. For that reason one tries to judge it on its own terms, by taking particular note of the way its refutation or confirmation becomes significant in the present.

But it is also appropriate to situate it within the historical period where it was born and developed, and to assess it with reference to its spatial, temporal and social co-ordinates.

If one is successful in this task, then one discovers that in general Hegel has suffered a great injustice. His memory has not always been treated with that fairness or generosity from which his contemporaries benefited.

It is as if there were two weights and two measures; every severe judgement collects, like thunder, to strike this highest point.

In the life and work of Hardenberg one easily finds plenty of unpleasant features. The Prussian chancellor neither espoused nor achieved ideas that were any more 'advanced' than those of Hegel. Yet everyone appreciates that he was a "reformer", or at least a "half-reformer" – a type of man quite rare in his day.

As for Altenstein, historians agree in calling him a "liberal" without quibbling over details.

Why, then, does Hegel emerge from the fray with fewer laurels? He shows himself to be no less an innovator than his protectors.

But we should also compare him with his friends. Varnhagen and Gans have acquired – with justice – the name of "people's friends". Yet the one they admired and loved, and from whom they drew their inspiration, has passed as an "enemy of the people"!

What praises are showered on Förster, Carové, and Cousin, who languished in the jails or were subjected to the insults of the Prussian police. But it is quite proper if one almost allows the responsibility for their persecutions to fall back on Hegel, when in fact he came to their defence, gave them assistance, and offered encouragement!

Hegel was just as worthy as those who received instruction in his classes, who were pleased to deserve his respect, who mourned his loss, and who published and propagated his ideas.

We have leafed through Hegel's file.

By restoring his true face, history offers us the opportunity to render him his due, and to recognize him for what he was.

Translator's Notes

(indicated by asterisks in the text)

(**page 9**) Introduced to Goethe in 1774 by von Knebel (their mutual friend), Karl August, the young hereditary prince of Saxe-Weimar, invited Goethe to Weimar, his capital, where he was soon enlisted into government. The poet thus played an important role in making the University of Jena, which was in the Duke's territories, the centre of German cultural life. Fichte, Schelling, the Schlegels and Hegel were among those who gravitated there in the period before Napoleon defeated the allied forces at the battle of Jena. As D'Hondt suggests (p. 85) Goethe played an active role in appointments and promotions, and continued to be closely associated with Knebel.

The Duke of Saxe-Weimar was noted for his liberal tendencies. On page 53 we find that a conversation with him got Johannes Schulze into difficulties with the Prussian authorities; on page 93 D'Hondt reports that the Duke continued to support the philosopher Fries, whom he was compelled by the Holy Alliance to dismiss from his university post; and he allowed the nationalist student demonstration to take place at the Wartburg. On page 123 he is reported to have intervened on behalf of the imprisoned student activist, Gustav Asverus.

Goethe, Knebel and Karl August, as well as many other liberal republicans mentioned by D'Hondt in these pages, are known to have been members of the Masonic Order. (See *Hegel secret.*)

(**page 9**) A colleague of Hegel's both as a student in Tübingen and at Jena, Niethammer left Saxe-Weimar to become Professor at Würzburg, and then, in 1808, a senior counsellor in the Ministry of Schools and Churches in Montgelas's administration at München. He used his influence to obtain for Hegel a post as editor of a newspaper in Bamberg, and later the headship of a secondary school in Nürnberg.

The elector of Bavaria, Maximilian IV, sympathized with the French in the wars of the period. As a result of this alliance, Bavaria acquired the bishoprics of Bamberg, Würzburg and Augsburg. The elector, soon to become King Maximilian I, appointed the francophile Max Josef von Montgelas, who initiated under pressure from Napoleon wide-ranging reforms. After Napoleon's fall, Montgelas was dismissed because he was not prepared to carry through with constitutional reforms. Maximilian continued to rule as a model constitutional monarch until his death in 1825.

(**page 10**) Peter Gabriel van Ghert was a Flemish Catholic who studied with Hegel during his years at Jena. "After his return to the Low Countries he held a number of important administrative appointments and supported a national reform of the educational system and church-state relations against the opposition of traditional privileged groups and demagogic manifestations of mass emotion." J.E. Toews, *Hegelianism* (Cambridge, 1980) 80.

(**page 15**) D'Hondt incorrectly names Hegel's mistress as *Christiane* Burckhardt. But H.S. Harris, who gives some details of the liaison that Hegel had with his promiscuous chambermaid, calls her Johanna, and says that her maiden name was Fischer. See *Hegel's Development: Night Thoughts (Jena 1801-1806)* (Oxford, 1983) lxvii-lxx.

(**pages 16, 23, 56**) D'Hondt frequently refers to a sentence from the Preface to the *Philosophy of Right*: "To recognize reason as the rose in the cross of the present and thereby to enjoy the present, this is the rational insight which reconciles us to the actual, the reconciliation which philosophy affords to those in whom there has once arisen an inner voice bidding them to comprehend, not only to dwell in what is substantive while still retaining subjective freedom, but also to possess subjective freedom while standing not in anything particular and accidental but in what exists absolutely." (Knox translation,

12) In his note Knox refers to the Rosicrucians, but a rose and cross were also combined in the Lutheran coat of arms.

(page 21)   Karl Reichsherr vom und zum Stein became Frederick William III's Minister of State on the insistence of Napoleon, and in that position implemented reforms in the political administration of Prussia. He employed the services of Schön, Scharnhorst and Gneisenau, among others. In 1807 he issued an edict for the ease of possession and free use of landed property, which freed the peasants from feudal servitude. He resigned in 1808, but continued to be active politically in Russia, and later in Westphalia.

(page 21, 50)   Gerhard J.D. von Scharnhorst collaborated with A.W. von Gneisenau to reorganize the Prussian army during the Napoleonic wars.

(page 26)   A general under the *ancien régime* in France, Lazare Nicolas Marguerite Carnot became an ardent republican in the French Revolution and later the general who made the revolutionary army into an effective fighting force. Subsequently a member of the Committee of Public Safety and one of the five Directors, he withdrew from active involvement when Napoleon assumed sole power in order to remain true to his republican (and therefore anti-imperialist) convictions. He emerged from retirement when France came under threat in 1814. After Waterloo he was sentenced to prison in the citadel at Magdeburg, and died there in 1823.

(page 27)   In the final chapter of *Hegel, philosophe de l'histoire vivante*, "Les Leçons de l'histoire," D'Hondt develops his arguments for this claim: "The great statesman educates himself, improves himself, and becomes cultured: this is quite different from learning lessons, placing all one's confidence in them, and being content simply to repeat them. He carries history further in accordance with the new standards that it has prescribed for him. Or rather, history carries itself forward in his person, develops as an autonomous entity (the universal spirit) or at least as a specific social reality." (446f) (**page 35**) In the French National Convention of 1792-97, the two clearly defined "parties" were the Jacobins, who advocated a unified, democratic state, and the Girondins, who wanted to limit the power of Paris with its mass movements and ensure the dominance of the middle class. Jacobins sat on the left side of the chamber, while the Girondins took their place on the right, thus bequeathing to posterity a pair of political categories. The extreme Jacobins, led by Robespierre, sat in the upper reaches of the banked seats, and were thus called the Montagnards, or the Mountain.

The Convention had succeeded the Legislative Assembly of 1791-2. There the two parties that dominated the Convention were grouped together as the republican party, or Jacobins. Apart from a few who wanted a return to the *ancien régime*, their opponents were those who advocated a constitutional monarchy, or the Feuillants.

Beyond French borders, Napoleon was seen as an emissary of the Revolution in its totality. Within France, his imperial pretensions set him against the democratic and republican forces.

(**page 39**) The theologian and church historian H.E.G. Paulus preceded Hegel to Jena, Bamberg and Nürnberg before becoming Professor of Theology at Heidelberg in 1810.

(**page 39**) B.G. von Niebuhr was a historian who served in Stein's ministry but resigned when Stein fell and became Professor at the new University of Berlin, from which position he supported the war of liberation against Napoleon.

(**page 44**) Theodor von Schön was a student of Kant's who became one of the most important figures in the reforming ministry of the Freiherr vom Stein.

(**page 50**) J.J. von Görres was an early supporter of the French Revolution, but became disillusioned, and shared with Ernst Moritz Arndt the role of publicist for the war of liberation against Napoleon. He ended his life as Professor of History at Munich.

(page 65) The date cited here by D'Hondt is a mistake. The dinner took place on March 5, 1830. See Marianne's diary for 6 March, 1830 in Hölderlin *Sämtliche Werke*, G.S.A., Band 7,3 p.119.

Despite Harris's comment in the Preface, the Prince William, whose wife was born Marianne von Hesse-Hombourg, was neither the crown prince, Frederick William, nor his brother, the future Kaiser William I. Most likely he was of the earlier generation.

D'Hondt provides us with more information on Isaac von Sinclair in *Hegel secret*. An associate of Johannes Schulze and an acquaintance of Hardenberg, he was the son of Alexander von Sinclair, tutor of Frederick V of Hesse-Hombourg, who was in turn the father of Princess Wilhelmina. Sinclair was known as a liberal. In company with the poet Hölderlin, he was threatened with prosecution for treason. Sinclair and Hölderlin were instrumental in finding Hegel a tutor's position in Frankfurt in 1797. When von Sinclair died in 1815, Hegel lost the last friend with whom he corresponded in familiar terms.

(page 76) Savigny appears several times in these pages, and not always as a reactionary. A professor at the University of Berlin, he contributed to the collection for the dismissed De Wette (page 112) and attended a student festival in company with Hegel (page 166).

(page 84) It was not by chance that the Wartburg was chosen as the place for the student demonstration of 1817, the three-hundredth anniversary of Luther's *95 Theses*. Luther had been kept under house arrest in this fortress in the tense days after the Diet of Worms, and had translated the New Testament there. In the Middle Ages it had been the site of the minstrel's contest immortalized in Wagner's *Tannhäuser*, as well as the home of St. Elizabeth of Hungary.

(page 102) Although originally a Swiss Huguenot, Henry-Benjamin Constant de Rebecque supported the French Revolution, only to be sent into exile by Napoleon. He shared his exile with Mme. de Staël, another important French liberal. In 1816 he returned to Paris and became a member of the opposition party.

(**page 107**) Engels's phrase "national uprising of 1813" refers to the popular war of liberation that arose throughout Germany against the Napoleonic occupation.

(**page 110**) In an essay, "L'histoire et les utopistes selon Hegel et Marx," reprinted in *De Hegel à Marx*, pp 135-163, D'Hondt expands on the connection made here between Schiller's Karl Moor (whose image lies behind Hegel's chapter in the *Phenomenology* on "The Law of the Heart and the Frenzy of Self-conceit") and Sand's assassination of Kotzebue. In the same context he introduces Hegel's aversion for Fries's sentimentalism.

(**Page 120**) In *Hegel's Development: Night Thoughts* (lxviii note) H.S. Harris remarks that Karl Hegel, in preparing the first edition of his father's letters, not only judiciously edited them to play down any suggestion of subversion (see in this volume, page 181), but also made some of the originals illegible. Harris speculates that others may well have been destroyed altogether.

(**page 147**) The Count von Schlabrendorff and K.E. Oelsner were central figures in the Girondin and Masonic connections that D'Hondt explores in *Hegel secret*. The Count's residence in Paris provided a place where liberals of central Europe could establish contact with the moderate republicans. (p. 14) A letter of 1794 from Hegel to Schelling reports the former's encounter with Oelsner, a Silesian, and refers to his "Letters" which had recounted events in Paris for the German readers of *Minerva*. (pp 7ff) Oelsner became a political refugee after the fall of the Girondins forced him to flee from Paris.

(**page 171**) "I think myself that the famous story of the planting of a 'tree of liberty' at Tübingen (in which Hegel was supposedly involved) originated from some ceremonial act on Bastille Day 1793 — probably a sort of Maypole dance around a pole or tree which was designated, for the occasion, as the 'Tree of Liberty'. It is quite certain that there was no actual tree planting, but it is equally certain that the rumour of one was spread at about this time, since the Ephor was obliged to contradict the story. Probably Hegel was not there, though, since other evidence indicates that he was at home for a considerable period during this, his last term at Tübingen." H.S. Harris, "Hegel and the French Revolution," *CLIO* vii, 1 (1977) 9.

(page 171) In 1798, after leaving Berne, Hegel anonymously published a translation of Jean-Jacques Cart's *Lettres confidentielles*, to which he added an introduction and notes. The full title suggests the polemical nature of the work: *Confidential Letters concerning the former constitutional relation of the Land of Vaud to the State of Berne. A complete exposition of the earlier oligarchy of the Berne nobility. Translated from the French of a deceased Swiss author and supplied with notes.* In the land of Vaud, lying within French territory, a popular uprising was crushed in 1792 by the Canton of Berne, which controlled its government. Despite Hegel's title, Cart was not dead at the time. His *Letters* had been published in 1793 after his flight to Paris. But he spent some time in North America before the Vaud was finally integrated into France and he was able to return in 1798.

The translation is known to be the work of Hegel only because it was listed under his name in Meusel's *Lexicon* of German writers in 1805. H.S. Harris suggests that the publication of the translation should be viewed as the first shot in a campaign for "justice" in Württemberg. (*Hegel's Development: Towards the Sunlight* (Oxford, 1972) 422)

(page 184) Ludwig Börne, a Jew born in Frankfurt, converted to Protestantism in 1817 to become eligible for public office. He was a vigorous opponent of the political and cultural reaction, and his *Letters from Paris* transmitted the ideas of French liberalism to Germany.

Index